A Tale of Five Cities

A Tale of Five Cities

A History of the Five Patriarchal Cities of the Early Church

JAY E. THOMPSON

WIPF & STOCK · Eugene, Oregon

A TALE OF FIVE CITIES
A History of the Five Patriarchal Cities of the Early Church

Wipf and Stock Publishers
199 W. 8th Av.e, Suite 3
Eugene, OR 97401

www.wipfandstock.com

ISBN 13: 978-1-60608-704-6

Manufactured in the U.S.A.

Contents

Acknowledgements

I WOULD LIKE TO acknowledge my dear friend and encourager Dr. James Gibson, Professor of Christian Counseling and Academic Dean of Faith Evangelical Seminary, for his tenacious words of encouragement through the research and writing of this book. There was not a day that I was without his friendly counsel and encouragement. Thank you, James.

I would also like to thank my dear friend Dr. Michael Adams, President of Faith Evangelical Seminary, for his support and patience while I was so deeply engaged in this project and for his allowing me the time to concentrate and focus for these years that I spent in this critical time period of history. Thank you, Mike.

1

Introduction to the History
of the Five Patriarchal Cities

A STUDY OF THE history of corporate worship and administration found in the five patriarchal cities of the early church in no way can be comprehensive. Where does one go to collect the historical data for such a project? How does one make the project a task that can be completed? How is worship distinguished from ritual, and administration from political gain and intrigue? In asking these questions the reader will perceive the monumental undertaking of the project.

It is best not to distinguish worship from ritual as a historical observer because in any form of corporate worship there will be individuals participating who are in every spiritual sense of the word "worshiping," and in the same setting, individuals who are "practicing ritual." The administration of the church is in like manner tightly related to and linked to worship, because the administration is the maintenance and control of the environment surrounding the corporate service of worship through doctrine, prayer, evangelism, and life conduct. Therefore, in order to introduce corporate worship and administration, I will draw some parameters for the study.

This research is confined to the history of church of the God of the canonized Christian Scriptures (66 books) as defined by the sixteenth-century Reformers, and that corporate worship and administration is identified by orthodoxy (biblical and historical). Attention may and must be given to some movements in history labeled as heresy. The historical time concern will concentrate from 35 CE to the sixth century CE.

To accomplish this great task I will focus my attention on the five primal church cities in which Christianity has its roots. Ultimately, the churches of most importance to history and which provide us tradition

1

and progress toward a worldwide evangelism are the five patriarchal churches identified from Constantine onward. These are Jerusalem from 35 CE to 115 CE, Antioch from 35 CE to 550 CE, Rome from 35 CE to 450 CE, Alexandria from 40 CE to 500 CE, and Constantinople from 323 CE to 550 CE. These churches represent the study of the transition from a Judaistic worship to a Gentile church form of worship and administration.

The method of my study takes a historical theological approach. Source material is used when possible. The writings of the church fathers are of particular importance and help to establish connection to the time that these churches were conducting their affairs in administration and worship. I do not attempt to analyze liturgies that were prevalent and in use in past days, except where they establish the orthodoxy of doctrine and practice for the whole of the church.

After defining the terms that are relevant in the Scriptures, I will establish the position that most of the churches in their settings contributed to the understanding that worship is a life experience, and that all that was done was to be a testimony to God and his righteousness. This was the understanding of the Greek philosophical schools. *Pistis and pisteuein* (faith and to believe) were always accompanied by the preposition *eis* (into). If I was a stoic philosopher, I believed *into* my system of thought, rhetoric, and life. If I was an Epicurean philosopher, I believed *into* my system of thought, rhetoric, and life. All those with whom I was in contact would know me by my philosophy. As soon as I opened my mouth in word, all those hearing me knew who I was. This Eastern (Hellenistic) concept of belief permeates the Eastern churches and establishes that all my acts are worship to my God whom I serve in *eusebeia* (piety). In contrast to the Hellenistic East was the Latin West, which believed *on*, or *unto* something. The foundation did not incorporate me into it but allowed me to jump on and off at will so that I lived two lives, the life of a believer and also the life of a secular citizen. In the East there was no distinction between secular and sacred.

WHAT IS WORSHIP IN THE HEBREW OLD TESTAMENT SCRIPTURES?

In the Old Testament there are three words commonly translated as "worship."

SHAHAH means to bow down, to prostrate oneself before another for the purpose of giving that one homage, honor, and reverence. This is a mode certainly indicating salutation, as the worshiper initially enters into the presence of the objective of worship. The act of greeting the one in authority by kneeling to the ground and touching one's forehead to the ground also invokes the image of this word. I must also confess that the word has been used historically in regard to a king-to-subject relation.

SeGID, in the Aramaic, refers also to the act of worship in the same way as the Hebrew word *SHAHAH*.

ASAB is a Hebrew word that means to carve, to labor, to serve an idol. The worship form of idolatry in the Hebrew mind begins with the making of the idol through carving or some other form of labor. The intent of the worship is to create the object that one will then serve in his labor.

In defining the word "worship" it is expedient also to distinguish between false practices of worship in the historical settings in which the words came forth. As *ASAB* means to carve, to labor, to serve an idol, there are two distinct criteria within the definition that point toward the falsity of the worship (*ASAB*). This term denotes that man has created the object of worship for his own edification, and such an object is the product of man's hands. The outcome of the planning process replaces the reverence and homage to the true God with the service to that "thing" which can be controlled, namely, man's own creation. Secondly, that man who created the image or object will serve the object in his labor whether the created object is physical or imagined.

We see in Exodus that the Law Moses receives is to be kept as a condition for "possessing" the land that the Israelites are given in fulfillment of the promise made to Abraham about the "ownership" of the land. A clear distinction will be made between these two covenants: The one is a promise to Abraham that YHWH would be God to "his descendants (seed)" and would "give" to Abraham's offspring the land of Abraham's sojourning (Canaan) (Gen 17:7–8). The sign of this "everlasting" covenant was circumcision. To the Jew, circumcision became a sign to the world that he was a part of the Hebrew race and a participator in the covenants with YHWH. It was also a sign to God that the Jew was obedient to that sign of circumcision and therefore could be allowed to approach YHWH through the interworkings of the priest and the sacrificial system affiliated with the temple that was given through Moses.

The second everlasting covenant is given through Moses, and does not nullify or add conditions to the first. Moses is given these words, "If you … keep My covenant, then you shall be My own possession among all the peoples for all the earth is mine; and you shall be to Me a kingdom of priests and a Holy nation" (Ex 19:6 ASV). Upon this the Law was given to Moses to speak to the people. He was asked to come up again taking with him Aaron, Nadab, Abihu, and the seventy elders of the tribes to worship at a distance, and it says "they saw the God of Israel; and under His feet there appeared to be a pavement of sapphire, as clear as the sky itself. Yet He did not stretch out His hand against the nobles of the sons of Israel; and they beheld God and they ate and drank" (Ex 24:10 NASB). From there Moses was summoned to the mountain and given the stone tablets and a large portion of the rest of the Law, including a pattern for making the sign of this covenant, the Ark and the tabernacle. These were the conditions for Israel to "possess" the land of Canaan, from which God himself would drive out its inhabitants.

As *SHAHAH* in Hebrew connotes that the individual is responding to or toward the one in the superior seat, be that a person of higher status or a being of superiority such as God. The key in the equation is individual, and not group, congregation, crowd, or corporation. Worship, then must be understood as the individual response to God. Be that as it may, observation of worship will never be perceived on the individual level, but on the corporate. So then, what is observed in the worship form is not the actual worship itself. To the Hebrew, the superior seat was in the "temple of the Lord." But as the prophet warned "Trust ye not in lying words, saying, 'The temple of the Lord, The temple of the Lord, The temple of the Lord, are these'" (Jer 7:4 KJV). In Israel it was easy to believe that the protection afforded to the nation was on account of the temple being in Jerusalem. So it was in Jerusalem at the ministry of Christ that the Jews put their faith and worship in the building and not the Lord. The worship revolved around it, and the nation was unable to function in their ritual and worship without it, yet the Lord had declared the temple to be "a house of prayer," *oikos proseuchēs* (Matt 21:13). The ministry of James as described by Heggesipus and recorded in Eusebius illustrates this point well: "he used to enter the temple alone and was often found kneeling and imploring the forgiveness for the people, so that his knees became hard like a camel's from his continual kneeling in worship to God and in prayer for the people."[1]

By the time of the destruction of the city and the temple, three sects of Jews were fighting each other for the possession of the temple, and they believed that the possession of it would make everything right, even the hatred of each other. There is a story in the Talmud about a servant who had misread the guest list of his master and invited a bar Kamza (the known enemy of the host) instead of his friend Kamza. When the day of the feast was at hand the enemy showed up at the banquet. The host, deeply riled by his enemy's presence, sought to remove him by force. Bar Kamza appealed to the host's sense of fair play saying that he should allow him to stay so as not to humiliate him before such important guests. Bar Kamza even negotiated and finally offered to pay for the entire banquet, but the host's hatred would not allow for any mercy, and the unwanted guest was thrown out of the banquet with due force. The rabbinic teachings attributed the destruction of the second temple in 70 CE to the host in this story and placed the blame on a certain Zechariah ben Abkilus, a leader of the zealots, who did not cast his vote to kill the bar Kamza and remove the defiling element from the temple.[2] But according to Josephus, because of the martyrdom of James the Just the destruction of the temple would not be postponed. He believed that the hatred of these three groups overwhelmed the compassion that God would have toward even his temple and therefore God had it destroyed because they had killed a holy man in the temple courtyard.

Once the temple was destroyed the Jewish Christians had some adjustments to make in regard to their connection to Judaism and the role they would play in Jerusalem. Not only was the temple a magnificent structure, but it was slated as a house of prayer. Christ states that emphatically. He said to them, "The Scriptures declare, 'My Temple will be called a house of prayer,' but you have turned it into a den of thieves!" (Matt 21:13 NLT). Twofold was his indictment of the priesthood servicing the temple. First, that prayer was the issue of the day for that was pleasing to God. Secondly, that the sacrificial system in the temple had been downgraded to "a den of thieves," and the state of the temple resources brought profit to the *archoi* (rulers) who did not necessarily conduct its business legally.

1. Heggisipus *Memoirs*, in Maier, *Eusebius*, 81.
2. Berman, "Kamza and Bar-Kamza."

If Christ's zeal for the temple was misplaced, then we have a problem with the bulk of the Old Testament passages about it. The emphasis on profit during the sacrificial ministry had overshadowed the temple as a "house of prayer." But the temple still functioned as a house of prayer during the early days of the church. "Peter and John went to the Temple one afternoon to take part in the three o'clock prayer service" (Acts 3:1 NLT).

With all the prayer taking place in the temple one might suspect that the Jews would recognize their Messiah, and yet they did not. Prayer was divided into two elements: the "Eulogies" or thanksgiving and the "*Tephillah*" or petition.[3] David metaphorically referred to his prayer in saying "let my prayer be set before You like incense" (Ps 141:2 NKJV), but in Christ's judgment their prayer was certainly not fragrant.

If prayer was the most elemental form of worship, then why was the temple destroyed if it functioned as a house of prayer? Paul brings into play another element that purifies "all things." He stated, "for every creature of God is good, and nothing is to be rejected, if it be received with thanksgiving: for it is sanctified through the word of God and prayer" (1 Tim 4:4–5 ASV). Paul confirms that the Word of God and prayer are united together in worship and are not to be separated from one another. Therefore, it is my impression that those who were given the ministry in the temple lacked the Word of God.

Keith Drury has written, "if Christians were forced by some despot to strip away the elements of worship one by one—singing, preaching, Communion, and so forth—prayer would likely be the last to go. For prayer may be the most elemental form of worship—of pledging allegiance to God and asking Him to act in our world."[4] On the contrary, it is my position that the Scripture directs the church to be students (disciples) of the Word of God. The acceptable form of worship as Paul instructed is the "renewing of the mind" (Rom 12:1). This renewing of the mind is accomplished by the Word of God and prayer as observed in 1 Timothy 4 so that prayer is not elemental to worship without the Word of God. The term Paul uses in Timothy is *enteuxis* (petition in the face of, or from an encounter with).[5] Paul incorporates in the same context the Jewish

---

3. Edersheim, *The Temple*, 119.

4. Drury, *Wonder of Worship*, 18.

5. Feyerabend, "ἔντευξις."

understanding of *eucharistos* (thanksgiving) as a point of invocation to bring about this encounter that is driven by the Word of God.

Unfortunately, the bulk of the Jerusalem-based Christians departed from the doctrines introduced by Paul in Antioch, and supposed that the God who came—the Son of God, the Word—was adopted by the Father as Son, and came to reform the Law because the temple was no more. This and other impieties early in church history caused a departure from the Word of God and separated these churches from its influence. Many of these newly formed Jewish churches (Ebionites) claimed apostleship from James the bishop of Jerusalem. They also declared Paul to be an apostate from the Law. Their scriptures were the *Apocryphon of James* and the *Gospel of the Holy Twelve*, which the churches that Paul had established considered to be contrary writings that promoted a Gnostic message.

The form of worship is the physical surroundings in which individual worship takes place. The physical environment for worship must be viewed as "promoting" true worship within an individual or the corporation. The service that is rendered or administration that is established serves to control the physical environment in which worship is accomplished. The temple in Jerusalem became the focal point of all Jewish worship, and it included a system of administration to perform the functions of service as far as the Jewish nation was concerned.

This alludes to the ability of judging or evaluating the control of the worship environment according to its degree of success in promoting the individual's engagement in worship as seen by the numbers within the corporation that do indeed respond in "spirit and in truth." It also gives us the ability to evaluate the motive of the form in its origins. The methodology of this research will be to observe historical events and theological teachings which impact the form of worship, evaluate its origin, purpose, and its effect on worship, and differentiate the form of worship between *SHAHAH* and *ASAB*.

WHAT IS WORSHIP IN THE NEW TESTAMENT?

The Hellenistic understanding of worship can clearly be seen by the words employed in the text of the New Testament and the Septuagint (the Greek translation of the Old Testament). Several New Testament words are affiliated with worship.

Eusebeia is related to the Greek secular term σέβομαι, meaning "to fall back before, to shrink from, to worship." *Eusebeian* is a way of life in regard to philosophy, which reflects the act that is done in direct response to the pantheon or the object of worship. This response is reflected in the relationships of family, husbands, wives, masters, slaves, legions, and imperator. The conception of the character of God became paramount to worship in the Gentile mode of Christian worship, because this has great impact on all of the relationships within the church.

Προσεύχομαι means "to pray" and is derived from the word ευ—"χομαι, meaning "to invoke a deity, to vow, to ask, to beseech, to pray, to dedicate." "It is true that many of the Greek gods bear in their names or attributes the signs of origination, in nature, in wood, in hill, in the weather or the cycle of the year."[6] The emphasis of which is the form of prayer in which one can invoke the god for favor in a certain substance, concerning a certain attribute, in regard to a certain elemental situation.[7] These prayers would task one god over the other depending on their strength over war, commerce, harvest, weather, nature, and one another. A prescription of words or liturgy was used to invoke the gods or God.

Προσκύνεω means "to fall down before, to worship, to revere, to prostrate before a higher authority." An illustration of *proskyneō* is seen in the Gospel of John. "But the hour cometh, and now is, when the true worshipers shall worship the Father in spirit and truth: for such doth the Father seek to be his worshipers" (John 4:23 ASV).

Συμβουλευω means "to counsel, advise, exhort, to consult together, plot." *Symbouleuō* is found in Revelation 3:18, "I counsel you to buy refined gold," and the noun form appears in Romans 11:34, meaning "counselor."

In the Septuagint, Isaiah 1:18 uses the word *dialegomai*: Come let us reason together says the Lord, "though your sins be as purple, I will make them white as snow, though they be as scarlet I will make white as wool" (author trans.).

Concerning corporate Christian worship, all things of the church are weighed by the head of the church, which is Christ Jesus. A literal translation of Romans 12:1 states, "Therefore, I call on [or, counsel with, go alongside] you, brothers, through the compassions of God, to present your bodies a living sacrifice, holy, acceptable to God [which is] your intel-

6. Greeven, "προσεύχομαι."

7. Ibid.

ligent, sacred service" (παρακάλω οὐν ὑμας ἀδελφοὶ δια τῶν οἰκτί ρμων τοῦ θεοῦ παραστῆσαι τα σώματα ὑμῶν θύσιαν ζῶσαν ἀγαίν εὐάρεστον τῷ θεῷ τὴν λογίκην λατρείαν ὑμῶν).

Paul called on the church of Rome for each person in the synagogue of believers to present oneself, παριστῆσαι (παριστῆαι, παριστάνω). This word is a compound word using the preposition πάρα and the verb ἵστημι, which literally means to make "to stand beside," that is, "(transitively) to *exhibit, proffer*, (specifically) *recommend*, (figuratively) *substantiate*; or (intransitively) to *be at hand* (or *ready*); *aid*: assist, bring before, command, commend, give presently, present, prove, provide, show, stand (before, by, here, up, with), yield."[8] This is their *latreia* (λατρείαν), their *ministration* of God, that is, *worship*: (divine) service.

Paul confirms that "to present" (to make to stand beside, to place beside) one's body as a living (not dead) sacrifice is one's logical (intelligent) divine worship or service. Because *histēmi* means "to make to stand," it has the connotation of being passive or being placed, being set, being appointed, so that one's body is appointed to be a sacrifice alive, not dead. This gives the understanding of physical call and appointment made by the head of the church, Jesus Christ, of all who are his. The church lives and breathes for Christ. The corporate body moves by the direction of Christ the head, and nothing is done in the church apart from that. This makes up the illustration of the church as a living and breathing body. That assures us that the history of church is directed and orchestrated by Christ. There is no good thing that is not made good in Christ, and there is no bad thing that isn't sanctified in Christ, because "all things work to the good to those who love God even those who are called according to His purpose" (Rom 8:28 NASB).

THE ADMINISTRATION OF WORSHIP

The intention of Scripture appeared to combine the Church and churches administratively to the form of worship. It became apparent that the administration of the church was also worship to God. The Greeks were able to visualize this connection because of the way the term *eusebeia* includes relationships here on the earth. The Jew, however, inferred that the worship of God was only directed toward God and not toward man, although

---

8. Reike, "παριστῆμι."

it could be directed toward Jews who were in need. Even that was not as evident, as James says to the Jews,

> Now listen! The rich [ones] weep, wail over your miseries, the ones coming upon [you]! Your riches have rotted, and your clothes have become moth-eaten. Your gold and silver have corroded, and their rust will be for a testimony against you and will consume your flesh as fire. You stored up [treasure] in the last days! Listen! The pay of the laborers, of the ones having cut down grain [in] your fields, their [pay] having been kept back by you cries out, and the shouts [or, outcry] of the ones having reaped have entered into the ears of the Lord of Armies [fig., the Lord Almighty]. You lived in luxury on the earth and were self-indulgent; you nourished [fig., fattened] your hearts as in a day of slaughter. (Jas 5:1–5)

Among the Jews to which James wrote there was evidence that even wages were being withheld from laborers and the poor were those who had jobs. If these to whom money is due are not cared for by the wealthy how much more the poor who had no job?

Diakonia means "service, ministry," and it is the word from which we get *deacon*. It is found in the Second Epistle to the Corinthians where Paul writes, because the *diakonia*, "ministry *[or, administration]* of this sacred service not only is supplying the needs of the holy ones but is also overflowing through many thanksgivings to God" (2 Cor 9:12).

Oikonomia appears in Ephesians 1:10: "with respect to the administration of the fullness [or, completion] of the times, to gather together all things in Christ, the things in the heavens and the things on the earth" (Eph 1:10). Paul wrote this to emphasize the point that the *oikonomia* of God would accomplish two goals: First, the completion of God's economy was to gather all things in Christ. This meant that redemption through Jesus Christ was not of humanity only, but designed to lift the whole of creation from the futility to which it had been subjected. Elsewhere he iterates, "For the earnest expectation of the creation eagerly awaits the revelation of the sons of God. For the creation was subjected to futility, not of its will, but because of the One having subjected [it] in confident expectation, because even the creation itself will be set free from the slavery of the corruption into the liberty of the glory of the children of God" (Rom 8:19–21). Second, the worship of God was accomplished by the Divine administration and would include the creation. "And you should not presume to be saying within yourselves, '[w]e have Abraham [as our] father,' for I say to you that God is able to raise children to Abraham out of these stones" (Matt 3:9). And also in Luke 19:39–40, "some of the Pharisees from the crowd said to Him, 'Teacher, rebuke Your disciples!' And answering, He said to them, "I say to you, if these shall be silent, the stones will cry out!" Clearly Christ has laid down the gauntlet to the Pharisees that those who should be worshipping the Son of God were the leaders (Scribes, Pharisees, and Sadducees), but there was no such worship in Jerusalem at that time. To confirm this Paul writes, "and to enlighten all *[as to]* what *[is]* the administration[9] of the secret, the one having been hidden from the ages in God, the One having created all things through Jesus Christ" (Eph 3:9).

THE GREEK CHRISTIANS SOUGHT TO COMBINE THE TWO AS ONE

Throughout the early years of the church, the Christians pondered the issues, how Judaistic should we be? How Hellenistic should we be? The two different perspectives of worship belong to the Judaistic pattern and the Hellenistic pattern. As we have observed by the definitions of the words employed in Scripture, Judaistic worship involves an approach to the God, the prostrating before the God, and the receiving of blessing from the God. It entails the hurrying toward visitation, only after the worshiper has fulfilled the letter of the Law and has been allowed to approach. The Hellenistic pagan worship viewed the gods as petty, malevolent, and evil. The worship entailed petition to entreat the god to depart from them, and after visitation, required *eusebeia* (piety) to prevent the god from returning and bringing calamity upon the population. The Hellenistic worship based its form of petition upon the calamities of the society or corporate order. Often the Greeks did not know which god they had offended. Their petition was directed to the oracles (in Delphi) in which large largeses were given to find which gods were offended and what particular sin or social impiety was being punished. To the Hellenist, sin or missing the mark was due to a public impiety (*ouk esti eusebeia*), a child being disrespectful to a parent, a slave to a master, a lord neglecting the needs of those he "owned." Such a calamity would bring about an inquiry, and a remedy for restoration of the *kosmos*, "order of things." By combining the two concepts of worship, the Hebrew form of drawing near to God in obedience to the

---

9. οἰκονόμια is used to convey economy, or house law.

Law and substituting faith for the Law so that the Gentile church sought to know God by the obedience of faith, the Christian is therefore restored to the *kosmos* and its relationships. To the "nation that was not a nation" and a "people who were not a people" (Rom 10:19) all things are restored to a point that history and day-to-day activity, the comings and goings, the mundane and spectacular are all part of worship, because through faith everything that is done is "wrought in God."

For the Jewish people the thing to be sought was a sign. The Hebrew population dispersed throughout the Mediterranean believed that if they received a sign from God it was because they had been obedient to the Law and performing its works. Paul brought this to bear when he wrote to the Corinthians; "Since also Jews ask for a sign, and Greeks seek wisdom" (1 Cor 1:22). He also distinguished the Greek in that the Hellenistic mind sought knowledge (*gnōsis*) and wisdom (*sophia*). These pursuits found their way into the Gentile church, and became points of boasting and arrogance of the flesh. This is evident in Paul's declaration:

> Since also Jews ask for a sign, and Greeks seek wisdom, but we proclaim Christ *[as]* having been crucified, to Jews indeed a stumbling-block and to Greeks foolishness, but to them, the ones called, both to Jews and to Greeks, Christ the power of God and the wisdom of God. Because the foolishness of God is wiser than people, and the weakness of God is stronger than people. For you see your calling, brothers *[and sisters]*, that *[there are]* not many wise according to *[the]* flesh, not many powerful, not many noble *[or, of high social status]*; but God chose the foolish *[things]* of the world, so that He should be humiliating the wise; and God chose the weak *[things]* of the world, so that He should be humiliating the strong; and God chose the insignificant *[things]* of the world and the *[things]* having been despised *[or, looked down on]*, and the *[things]* not being, so that He should nullify the *[things]* being *[fig., which exist]*, in order that all flesh shall not *[or, no flesh shall]* boast before God. (1 Cor 1:22–29)

Yet there is the strong inference that these groups need these yearnings. The focus of the Greeks in their quest for wisdom and knowledge and the focus of the Jews in their quest for a sign was to be under the condition that "by Him you are in Christ Jesus, who became to us wisdom from God, and righteousness and sanctification and redemption, so that, just as it has been written, The one boasting, let him be boasting in *[the]* Lord" (1 Cor 1:30). In order to bring the two groups together as one body, he chose to be the provider of the things they sought. In so doing he brought to the church "boasting in the Lord," or as we proclaim in American evangelical church circles, "it is not about me, it is about the Lord."

The Gentile (Greek) church would make its way in history and revolve around its yearning after wisdom. The church looked toward knowledge and wisdom in theology, anthropology, sciences, and arts. The Jewish church would seek signs and wonders, and be charismatic by its nature. The problem the church faced was the combination of the two goals, which became both divisive and destructive to the unity and the bonds that the two groups were required to maintain by command of the Lord. The prophets who provided the signs and wonders to the early church became odious to the teachers of theology, because they did not fit in the scheme of organization Paul had set.

The teachers and pastors feared for the unity of the flock and its survival in the Roman pagan world. Because of the free-wheeling and roving nature of the prophetic gift, the pastors and teachers found their communities disrupted by the prophetic messages. Whole church populations were cast into chaos by "thus saith the Lord," to the chagrin of the church leaders consisting of the offices of *episkopos*, *presbyteros* and *presbytera*, *diakonos* and *diakona*. Therefore, the leadership of the local bodies of believers developed liturgies and rules to govern the gifts to the churches. The *Didache*, which can be described as a book of order and a published book of liturgical services for the early-second-century churches (Syria and Asia Minor) mandated that the prophets could not speak for personal gain and were not to stay more than two days in a city.

Another cause for concern was the churches that were springing up following a man who claimed to be something great, claiming to be the Messiah. Men like bar Kokhba, who led the last revolt of the Jews against the Roman legions of Hadrian, or Montanus, the second-century prophet who by his charismatic gifts sent the churches of Asia Minor into confusion. Such men and many more traveled through the regions gathering followers to themselves with contrary doctrines. Against these the orthodox leaders contended. Because of the plethora of contrary doctrines that came with false Christology and maligned the way of salvation, the bishops of orthodox churches gathered together to review and judge the doctrines by their merit and truth to the apostolic teachings. Referring themselves to the Rule of Faith that was passed down from the apostles, they raised the need to declare the canon of Scriptures for teaching and reproof in the body of believers. Schools were formed to teach the science and art of interpretation (*hermeneutica*) as delivered by the apostles. By the middle of the third century there were two distinct schools of interpretation of Holy Scripture: Antioch, where those of faith were first called χριστιανοί, and Alexandria, where the Hellenistic Jewish philosopher Philo left his indelible mark.

However, the flesh is seen in historical events, and seldom does the historian record intent objectively, but must be speculative in his interpretation of the events that have taken place. Nor does the historian record character. His best ally should be the writings of those whom he wishes to understand. Events are important to the historical narrative, but are not the whole of the story. There is a lack in most narratives to connect the account to or discern behind the event either a spiritual cause or a human product of sin. The Hellenistic theists (Plato, Aristotle) sought to understand the prime cause or the "Unmoved Mover" and therefore explained the physical universe as just a shadow of the real and the spiritual. Because history is certainly a study of human events, the observer of history and the reader of accounts enter into a philosophy, a science, and an art of *hermeneutica*. Even in the case of most heretics who have been condemned, our only record of what they wrote and taught is provided by their accusers and in many instances their writings have been destroyed.

I will be focusing on the five patriarchal cities of great influence in the early church, where the history of Christianity unfolds in a colorful panorama of God-controlled and human politics, of human manipulation and individual and corporate sins. Yet the ultimate victory is won by God. I will look at the corporate and individual contributions that make those five churches special in history and unique in authority.

THE USE OF SYMBOLS IN WORSHIP

The use of symbols in church worship has an entirely different origin in the West than in the East. In Constantinople and Antioch, for instance, the symbol became a point for control of the physical environment to bring the mind or soul of the congregation to think on the divine things. The symbols were used to reference historical events, to remember the things of Christ. The orthodox position was based on the two separate natures of Christ. The physical-human aspect symbolized his humanity and the theological doctrine concerned the worship of the divinity.[10] The orthodox theologians surmised that since the Lord Jesus Christ accepted worship in the flesh then the symbols of physical things could also be objects of remembrance and totally acceptable in service and worship if it is known that the One true God is held up in its service. Behind every icon or symbol was a doctrine of orthodox theology. In the East, therefore, education became paramount, and everyone was a theologian.

However, in the West the symbols became objects of worship in a replacement (vicar) for the pagan background and Roman polytheistic religion. Christianity and its symbols were only a mere storefront for the old religion of Rome as supported and upheld by the caesars who held the office of Pontifex Maximus. The supreme position of the caesars was the foundation for the Roman Catholic position.

THE COMMONALITY OF THE FIVE CITIES

The common factors in the early patriarchal cities were the Rule of Faith in confession and the organization in administration or economy (*oikonomia*). All of the orthodox fathers worked according to the Rule of Faith that held a tie to the apostolic teaching of Peter, Paul, and John, particularly. The Rule of Faith was defined differently by many, but centered on the primary doctrines of the early church. This took two forms: the theological doctrine and the Scripture. On the theological subjects questions emerged in Christology, soteriology, eschatology, and later pneumatology, and anthropology. The scriptural field included canonicity and hermeneutics.

ESTABLISHMENT OF ORGANIZATION IN HISTORY AND WORSHIP

"Just as I urged you to remain in Ephesus while I traveled to Macedonia, so that you should give strict orders to certain [ones] to stop teaching a different [or, heretical] doctrine" (1 Tim 1:3). Paul had established the *episkopos* in Ephesus at his own authority as apostle to the Gentiles through Timothy as his lieutenant. Timothy's charge was to prevent some men from teaching strange doctrines. These doctrines were probably of

---

10. For every symbol in the East there was a story of divine intervention that brought the congregation to joint worship of the one true triune God. The recollection of such interventions could bring about a reoccurrence in history.

the Gnostic groups whose leaders presented themselves as apostles and their heresies as the "rule of faith." They could have been from a Jewish background such as the seven sons of the priestly Sceva found in Acts 19:14. Nevertheless, the organization of the church was so tightly connected to worship in doctrine and by the authority given to Timothy that the form of worship was measured by the Scriptures through sound hermeneutics. This became the very authority for all church activity in worship and administration in the East. As Paul states to Timothy in connection to the description of the qualifications for the *episkopos*, πιστός ὁ λόγος, "faithful is the word." There is no authority given to the church of Christ that is greater than the Scriptures. All ministry and service, all worship is driven by the authority of God's Word through the sixty-six writings of the Holy Bible. There is no other source for our worship and administration. The East confirmed the authority of the Scriptures through the general councils that canonized those books of the Bible that the church from its beginnings had recognized as having emanated from men (eyewitnesses) carried by the "Holy Spirit sent from God" (2 Pet 1:20–21). In contrast, the authority of worship and administration in the West was not centered on the authority of the Bible but on the authority of the bishop of Rome.

In setting up the qualities for the offices in the churches, Paul distinguished these officers as the instrument and administration to promote godly doctrine and curb insane and heretical speculation that has no purpose in "furthering the administration of God."[11]

HERMENEUTICS IN HISTORY AND WORSHIP
(HILLEL AND PHILO)

In the church, hermeneutics, which is the science of interpretation, refers to biblical hermeneutics. But it has also the aspect of art in that it requires skills. So then hermeneutics is the science and art of interpretation. When applied to the Bible, a scientific approach to interpretation becomes imperative. *Hermeneutics* comes from the Greek word *hermeneuō*, meaning "to explain, interpret, and translate." It is used several times in Scripture (John 1:39, 43; 9:7; 1 Cor 14:26, 2; Heb 7:28). The disciplines involved

---

11. 1 Tim 1:4 "and to stop paying attention to myths and endless genealogies, which cause disputes rather than [furthering the] administration [or, plan] of God, the [one] in faith" (ALT).

in biblical studies are grammar, history, and theology. The two historical schools of hermeneutics were located in Antioch and Alexandria. Antioch took on the skills and science of Paul and utilized the literal grammatical approach through the teacher of the Jews, Hillel. Alexandria inherited the allegorical approach to interpretation from Philo, Clement, and Origen. The contention that these opposite schools faced later in history became the very thing of which wars were made, as we will observe, and which divided the East from the West

CONFESSION OF FAITH AS WORSHIP
("WE BELIEVE" EAST AND "I BELIEVE" WEST)

Early in the church when there was unity between East and West, the churches viewed the creed as a common confession of faith, known and recited collectively in the corporate worship service. Hence the Nicene Creed started out saying "We believe." *Pisteuomen* was used to incorporate the creed for all those who were of the orthodox faith. Later in the West, the Council of Toledo (589) made the distinction of individual participation in the creed and started the creed with "I believe," as well as adding the controversial *filioque* clause.

Twofold was the discrepancy between the West and the East. The "I believe" clause connoted that the Church of Rome was under compulsion to follow the one man who was supreme, the pope, while the East reached agreement in creed by assembly and utilized the general councils to seek the truth of any matter that might come into contention with the doctrinal unity of the church. Second, the theologians in the East interpreted the *filioque* clause and they objected to the teaching it espoused, as conflicting with the biblical authority, and accepted doctrine conforming to the Rule of Faith. The Eastern theologians said that for the Holy Spirit to proceed from the Father and the Son there would have to be two sources that were divine, whereas in the one God there can only be one source of divinity or deity, and that the Father and Son are *homoousias* with each other, therefore there is only one source for the Holy Spirit who is also *homoousias* with both. The West responded in a trite way. It was called a "mystery" and therefore could not be understood by the common man, but only by the "Vicar" of Christ. Others from the West side-stepped the issue and, although agreeing with the Eastern theologians, they took a posture of "it doesn't really matter."

INVOCATION OF GOD BY ATTRIBUTES AND BY ACTIVITY, CHRISTOLOGY AND SOTERIOLOGY

The Greek Church sought to know the God that it would serve for eternity. The invocation toward that God was designed from the ancient pantheon to appease the deity into non-visitation, whereas the church of Christ was to eagerly await his coming, as John wrote, "Even so, Come, Lord Jesus" (Rev 22:20). Liturgies incorporated the attributes and activities of the Christ that it invoked to come. Therefore the East felt it necessary to be accurate about those attributes and activities. Theology became the essential science of the early Eastern Church. Supremacy of government became the essential science of the West.

2

The Jerusalem Church Model
(35 CE–70 CE)

THE EARLIEST CHRISTIAN CHURCH was the church in Jerusalem. Its inception began before Pentecost, just after Christ's crucifixion and resurrection had been accomplished. With a population of one hundred and twenty, they laid low, waiting for what the Lord had promised, the "power from on high." The Lord spent forty days "presenting Himself alive . . . by convincing proofs . . . and speaking to them of the kingdom of God" (Acts 1:3, author trans.). The Scripture says, "He gathered them together" and commanded them to not leave Jerusalem. Immediately, we see organizational needs being accomplished as Peter takes the lead when, by the interpretation of the Scripture, he initiated the appointment of a replacement apostle for Judas Iscariot. At this early stage of church history the societal living situation and the church were nearly indistinguishable because the disciples were meeting in homes, if not one home.

The upper room, we are told, was the place for their community. According to Merrill Unger, the upper room was the summer parlor or loft that was used by the wealthy for receiving company in small and large groups, and serving as family living quarters during the hot summer months. It has also been noted as the "chamber over the gate" where all the business and commerce of the city took place by the most prominent of citizens.[1] The city was divided into guild sections, each street and each quarter was segregated for the purpose of like commodity trades and for conducting the affairs pertinent for each trade. The gate area was the location where the "elders of the people" would gather to discuss news of the day, greet dignitaries from abroad, and make public announcements

---

1. Unger, *Unger's Bible Dictionary*, 1126.

affecting the government of the city.[2] For the next few weeks the church would live there, pray there and conduct business there.

We must ask certain questions before continuing to develop the worship portfolio of the Jerusalem church. How is it that the refugees of a leaderless "cult" obtained the most prominent housing in Jerusalem, and for that point in any city? During the Hellenistic economic period the upper room was the control and command center for the wealthiest of persons in the city, as it was situated directly over the main gate, having access to the approach of all trade caravans into the city and access to all the streets of city commerce, which were controlled by the various guilds.[3] From that vantage point the owner and wealthiest man in the city could identify trade trends and individuals of particular interest as future trade partners, to wine and dine them and house them in the finest digs in the city, the "upper room." Who was it in Jerusalem who owned the "Upper Room?" Are there some links that we might find in the Gospel accounts? I will endeavor to answer these questions and more.

In the writings of Josephus we learn that his father, Matthias, was one of the three most prominent men in Jerusalem. His lineage was noble, through the Hasmonean dynasty, being in the direct lineage of the daughter of Jonathan Hyrcanus.[4] Josephus also provides many insights into his role and his part in the history of the Jews. He declares himself to be of the high priestly line (Zadok) through his mother's lineage, as proscribed by Jewish law, which "made provision that the stock of the priests should continue unmixed and pure; for he who is partaker of the priesthood must propagate of a wife of the same nation, without having any regard to money, or any other dignities; but is to make scrutiny and take his wife's genealogy from the ancient tables and procure any witnesses to it."[5] After the captivity, the course of Jedaiah was the first and primary course of the twenty-four because it was the course of the high priesthood. According to Edersheim only four courses returned from captivity. Lots were drawn (five for each course) to fill the twenty courses that did not return. The particular line of the high priesthood remained with the Jedaiah course

2. Edersheim, *Sketches of Jewish Social Life*, 86.

3. This would correspond to the Damascus gate and the upper room over the gate connected all the guild streets to the two major trade routes entering the city from the north.

4. Josephus *The Life* 2–4 (Loeb, 5).

5. Josephus *Against Apion* 1.7 (author's trans.).

containing the lineage of Zadok and Abiathar (this was the first course).[6] Josephus claimed: "But my family is not only out of priests, but also out of the first class (or course) of priests out of the twenty-four."[7]

The family owned properties in Alexandria, making Josephus a citizen of Rome.[8] Matthias, being one of the three most prominent men in Jerusalem, undoubtedly had access to, if not ownership of the "upper room." Could this be the Matthias who was selected by lot in Acts 1 as the twelfth apostle? In Eusebius we find that Matthias was chosen, "To administer the common fund."[9] Wouldn't it make perfect sense that the man for the job of administering the common fund would be one of the most economically powerful men in Jerusalem?

In the historical narratives of Josephus, he presents three philosophical sects in Israel, that of the Pharisees, the Sadducees, and the Essenes.[10] The majority of the narratives covering this era, however, completely ignore the Essene sect, as if it either did not exist or was ignored. We will discuss this at greater length later.

In the earliest stages of the Jerusalem church, four corporate events transpired that gave rise to the form of worship that has endured throughout the history of the universal church to the current day.

THE SYNAGOGUE OF BELIEVERS

"They were all gathered together in one place" (Acts 2:1). The Lord himself had gathered all those who believed to the one place to wait. The purpose for their wait was to be together when the Father's promise came to fruition. By being in one place the effects of the promise would be clearly seen by the Jerusalem population. There appears to be a twofold purpose for a unified gathering of believers: The church gathers together to benefit from the presence of the Lord, and the church by gathering together becomes a

6. Edersheim, *The Temple*, 59.

7. Josephus *The Life* 2; author translation: ἔμοι δ οὐ Μόνον ἐξ ἱερων ἐστιν το γένον, ἀλλά καί ἐκ τῆν πρωτῆν ἐφημερίδον τῶν εἰκοσιτεσσάρων.

8. There were two provincial types in the Roman Empire, the empirical province and the senatorial province. The empirical province status granted Roman citizenship to landowners. Egypt was an empirical province of which Alexandria was one of the chief cities. Cilicia was another empirical province of which Tarsus was the chief city, making the apostle Paul a citizen.

9. Maier, *Eusebius*, 57.

10. Josephus *The Life* 2.

testimony to the nations. This passage employs the term *homou* to depict that all the believers were together in the same place at the same time.

UNITY IN PRAYER

"These all with one mind were continually devoting themselves to prayer." (Acts 1:14). After Christ had ascended, the church did not know for sure what to expect. The term translated as "with one mind" is *homothumadon*, a compound word from ὁμός and θύμος depicting "same" and "mental emotion" most occurrences in Greek literature are involved with anger, wrath, rage. If we look at the context of the passage, the culmination of intense unified emotion and prayer brought about the understanding of replacing the office of apostle left by the betrayer.

It was not obvious to any of the 120 what was to take place. As a result of the intense focus and anger over losing their mentor, Peter steps up to interpret the passages in the Psalms as being fulfilled that said his office would be given to another. This focus toward unity in intense thought and emotion brings about the first organizational change in the new church. As a result, the "twelve" are reinstated by the election of Mattathias (or Matthias) to replace the deposed Judas.

THE INTERPRETATION OF BIBLICAL TEXT
AND SCRIPTURAL READING (ACTS 1:15–26)

One of the very essential portions of the form of worship is the public reading of Scripture and its interpretation (the preaching and the teaching of the biblical text). In the early Jerusalem church the reading and interpretation of the Scripture becomes pertinent even before the appearance of the power that the church has been gathered to wait for. We find that as the disciples observed and participated in the teaching ministry of Jesus Christ, questions arose over proper interpretation of his teachings. In Matthew 13, after his discourse on the parables of the soils it says, "the disciples came to Him saying, 'Why do you speak to them in parables?' ... He answered ... 'to you it has been granted to know the mysteries of the kingdom of heaven, but to them it has not been granted.... Therefore, I speak to them in parables; because while seeing they do not see, and while hearing they do not hear nor do they understand. In their case the prophecy of Isaiah is being fulfilled'" (Matt 13:10–15 NASB).

We recognize two essential parts of this worship form:

1. The church was called to know the mysteries of the kingdom of heaven, but the world was not.

2. Proper interpretation of the mysteries is given by the choice of God, not the choice of men. Ultimately, this provides to the universal church in history a means by which the truth can be known and can be measured (the canon). The proper interpretation of the Hebrew Scriptures was going to lie in the building up of a few chosen men (apostleship) to propagate the truth of the testimony of Jesus Christ, and the establishment of proper hermeneutics in Old Testament and New Testament Scriptures. This has been called the rule of faith or analogy of faith.

Whereas the essentials of Jewish worship revolved around the Torah, in Christ the worship would revolve around its fulfillment through Jesus Christ. In the words of Rabbi Hanania ben Teradon:

> When *two* sit together and do not discuss words of Torah,
> this case is a session of scoffers, as it is said:
> —*'nor does he sit in the seat of scoffers'* (Ps 1:1).
> But when two sit and there are words of Torah between them,
> the Presence [*Shekinah*] dwells among them. (*m. Aboth* 3:2)

Also according to Rabbi Simeon ben Jo Hai:

> —"When *three* eat at one table and words of Torah are not spoken there,
> it is as if they ate at the altars of the dead, as it is said:
> —*'For all their tables are full of vomit and waste,*
> *there is no God* Heb: *maqom*; lit: "place" . . .' Isa 28:8.
> But when three eat at one table and bring up words of Torah,
> it is as if they ate from the table of God (*maqom*), blessed be He!
> [A]s it is said: "*And he said to me:*
> *This is the table that is before the Lord*' (Ezek 41:22)."
> (*m. Aboth* 3:3)

On the other hand Christ told his disciples, "Where two or three are gathered together in My name, there I am in their midst" (Matthew 18:20 NASB). The church in Jerusalem took a middle road position between the rabbis and the metaphysical presence of Christ in the gathering. Essentially, the church in Jerusalem would interpret the Old Testament Scripture in regard to the fulfillment that is in Christ, and there lies the presence of the Lord.

There was also an element of the teachings that permeated the Essene Jewish community. These appeared in the earliest of hermeneutics where Peter took the lead, but Peter learned these by experience. In the account in Acts 3:1—4:31 Peter and John are going up to the temple ἐπί τὴν ὥραν τῆς προσευχῆς τὴν ἐνάτην, "upon the ninth hour of the prayer." Peter and John understood the importance of prayer and yet were reluctant to enter the temple until the ninth hour of prayer. According to A. T. Robertson, there were three times of prayer in the temple, at the third hour, at the sixth hour, and the ninth hour (about three p.m.).[11] Luke's emphasis on the ninth hour of prayer signifies the purpose for which Peter and John venture. They enter not for sacrifice, but for prayer.

The appointment of service by lot fell on a member of the priestly family to enter the holy place, where "before him ... towards the heavy veil that hung before the Holy of Holies, was the golden alter of incense, on which the red coals glowed," and he would wait until given the "special signal" to "spread the incense on the altar, as near as possible to the Holy of Holies."[12] Then the congregation of Israel silently watched as their prayers rose to heaven in the cloud of incense. It was for this that Peter and John joined with the rest of Jerusalem at this hour of prayer to God. Even before the two were able to enter to pray, a certain man lame from his mother's womb being carried daily to the door to the temple to beg for alms captured the attention of Peter and John (Acts 3:2–4). Through this beggar the Lord provided Peter the opportunity to preach to all Jerusalem who had run out of the assembly of prayer to see Peter, John, and the one whom they knew "born lame" clinging to the disciples on two good and strong legs. The temple, as Peter would soon find out, was a place of opportunity for teaching and not the house of prayer that existed before and during the ministry of Jesus Christ.

THE NECESSITY FOR ORGANIZATION TO MEET PHYSICAL AND SPIRITUAL NEEDS IN A CORPORATE CHURCH SETTING (ACTS 4:25–28)

After unity of thought in angst and prayer, it became apparent to Peter by the Holy Spirit that there existed a need to appoint an apostle to replace Judas. It says,

11. Robertson, *Acts*, 53.

12. Edersheim, *Life and Times of Jesus the Messiah*, 139.

> In those days Peter stood up in the midst of the disciples (altogether the number of names was about a hundred and twenty), and said, "Men and brethren, this Scripture had to be fulfilled, which the Holy Spirit spoke before by the mouth of David concerning Judas, who became a guide to those who arrested Jesus. For he was numbered among us and was allotted his share in this ministry."
>
> (Now this man purchased a field with the wages of iniquity; and falling headlong, he burst open in the middle and all his entrails gushed out. And it became known to all those dwelling in Jerusalem; so that field is called in their own language, Akel Dama, that is, Field of Blood.) For it is written in the book of Psalms: 'Let his dwelling place be desolate, And let no one live in it'; and, 'Let another take his office.' Therefore, of these men who have accompanied us all the time that the Lord Jesus went in and out among us, beginning from the baptism of John to that day when He was taken up from us, one of these must become a witness with us of His resurrection. And they proposed two: Joseph called Barsabas, who was surnamed Justus, and Matthias. And they prayed and said, You, O Lord, who know the hearts of all, show which of these two You have chosen to take part in this ministry and apostleship from which Judas by transgression fell, that he might go to his own place." And they cast their lots, and the lot fell on Matthias. And he was numbered with the eleven apostles. (Acts 1:15–26 RSV)

This is not endorsing church bingo, but demonstrates the necessity for the organization to meet physical and spiritual needs in a corporate setting. Where the organization is not meeting the spiritual and physical needs, the organization is obligated to change to meet them, and in this instance it was mandated by Scripture. A clearer picture is presented of this principal of organizational service when a need arises in a cultural subgroup and the appointment of deacons is accomplished in Acts 6:1–8,

> Now in those days, when *the number of* the disciples was multiplying, there arose a complaint against the Hebrews by the Hellenists, because their widows were neglected in the daily distribution. Then the twelve summoned the multitude of the disciples and said, "It is not desirable that we should leave the word of God and serve tables. "Therefore, brethren, seek out from among you seven men of *good* reputation, full of the Holy Spirit and wisdom, whom we may appoint over this business; "but we will give ourselves continually to prayer and to the ministry of the word." And the saying pleased the whole multitude. And they chose Stephen, a man full of faith and the Holy Spirit, and Philip, Prochorus, Nicanor,

> Timon, Parmenas, and Nicolas, a proselyte from Antioch, whom
> they set before the apostles; and when they had prayed, they laid
> hands on them. Then the word of God spread, and the number of
> the disciples multiplied greatly in Jerusalem, and a great many of
> the priests were obedient to the faith. (Acts 6:1–8)

There are two telling words in the Acts 6 passage that allude to the
Hebrew prejudices being exercised in the Jerusalem church. Luke employs the word παραθεωροῦντο, which means to compare two things
side by side and determine one to be of less value than the other and to
be ignored. This brings light to attitude of disdain in the early church
toward the Hellenistic Jews and its propagation even among the twelve.
The second word employed by Luke is one that combines the word for
"table," τραπέζεις, with the term "serve," διακονεῖν. The twelve echo this
sentiment not by serving the Hellenistic Jews, but by stating "to serve
the tables." This being direct discourse, it is easy to see that Luke had
something to point out in the narrative by the reference to "tables" over
"Hellenists." Later, God gave Peter the vision of the unclean things in reference to the Gentiles being incorporated into his plan of salvation with
no particular sympathy toward the prejudices that were enduring in the
Jerusalem church. The God of the Jews was equalizing the playing field in
regard to salvation.

So intense was the prejudice of the Judean Jews that after work was
complete in the temple on the part of some of the skilled Alexandrian
Jews, those "true" Jews tore down the work and rebuilt it using natural
Judean Jews, fearing that the smoke of incense would go up to God in a
crooked column where the Alexandrians labored.[13] Edersheim develops
the understanding and reasons of such a prejudice in the community
of Jerusalem as he describes life at the time of Hillel. Sebua, "one of the
three wealthy men of Jerusalem," was a Jew of Alexandria, and many of
the Jews of Alexandria were "the richest and most influential."[14] There
obviously arose a great jealousy on the part of the natural Jews.[15] The
Alexandrian Jewish artisans were superior (case in point: the temple of
Onias at Leontopolis and the synagogue of Alexandria were the finest

13. Edersheim, *The Temple*, 179.

14. Ibid., 189.

15. A natural Jew was at least third generation residing in Judea and speaking Hebrew
as the primary tongue. They were also referred to as Hebrews in Acts 6:1 and distinguished from the Hellenists.

Jewish examples of craftsmanship and architecture in the entire world), and the Alexandrian Jewish business prowess dominated the Jerusalem economy.

At the time of Christ, there were more than one million Jewish men in Egypt, and over a third of the total population of Alexandria was prospering from business relations in Judea, Decapolis, Galilee, and Syria. The Alexandrian Jews at the time of Christ had every advantage in the Roman Empire, being citizens of Rome. (The citizen of Rome was encouraged to colonize newly acquired provinces).[16] It might be noted here that the Hebrew in Jerusalem was averse to commerce, as Edersheim writes, "We know in what low esteem peddlers were held by the Jewish authorities. But even commerce was not much more highly regarded."[17] This gave the Hellenistic Jews opportunity to prosper all that much more in Jerusalem. The Hebrews of Jerusalem would find themselves by necessity conducting commerce as part of unified Eastern provinces of the Roman Empire with an established infrastructure in roadways and Hellenistic commerce. The Hellenistic Jews found themselves in an advantageous position to supply goods and services to a Hebrew clientele who would have no dealings with Gentiles. The playing field was then leveled in two ways by the sovereign God, in soteriology and in economics.

RESTORING THE JEWISH PREJUDICES

Jewish prejudices toward the Gentiles were much reduced within the Essene sects. In a translation of the Geneza A document we read,

> Let no one attack any of the Gentiles with the intent to kill for the sake of wealth and spoil, nor may anyone carry away their wealth so that they may not blaspheme except by a counsel of the commonwealth of Israel. No one may sell a clean animal or bird to the Gentiles, lest they sacrifice them to idols; neither from his threshing floor or from his winepress shall he to sell to them, in all his property; his servant and his maidservant he may not sell to them, if they have entered with him to Abraham's covenant.[18]

Whereas the sect of the Pharisees had practiced strict separation from all contact with the Gentiles, some, and I must say most, Essenes

16. Unger, *Unger's Bible Dictionary*, 37.

17. Edersheim, *The Temple*, 187.

18. Wise, Abegg, and Cook, *The Dead Sea Scrolls*, 70.

allowed contact with the Gentiles. The intensity of this strict separation was even felt at all levels of ministry of the Jerusalem church. The process of restoring the church of Jerusalem back into the fold of the Judaistic society and the temple cult is twofold. The impact of the Jerusalem church primarily made up of Essenes would be reduced, or eliminated, and the church would be made acceptable to the Sanhedrin and to the temple leadership.

Because the Essene community had no particular tie to the temple in Jerusalem the true make-up of the Jerusalem church can be seen, as we follow the demographics of its growth. At the ascension of Christ there were 120 believers. On the day of Pentecost, fifty days after Christ's crucifixion, 3,000 were added to the number of the believers. There were at that time 3,120 members according to Acts 2:41, as it says, "They then that received his word were baptized: and there were added *unto them* in that day about three thousand souls" (ASV). As we continue, it says in Acts 2:47, "And the Lord added to them day by day those that were saved." We can conservatively estimate that number at one hundred per day. Therefore, by day sixty after the crucifixion there would be about 4,120 persons in the church of Jerusalem.

Shortly thereafter, we see another 5,000 men added to the number of the believing church of Jerusalem, as we read, "But many of them that heard the word believed; and the number of the men came to be about five thousand" (Acts 4:4 author trans.). If we factor women and children into the census, conservatively, we see 15,000 members added to the church, bringing the total to 19,120 and growing with every day: "and believers were the more added to the Lord, multitudes both of men and women" (Acts 5:14 ASV). So then at about day seventy after the crucifixion of Christ the church in Jerusalem numbered in excess of 20,000, but that was soon to change.

"And Saul was consenting to his death. And there began on that day a great persecution upon the church which was in Jerusalem; and they were all scattered abroad throughout the regions of Judaea and Samaria, except the apostles" (Acts 8:1 author trans.). On the theoretic seventy-first day of the church only twelve remain in Jerusalem. Because the majority population of the church in Jerusalem was of the Essene sect, their tie to the temple is negligible.[19] Therefore, they were dispersed to Damascus

19. The Essenes believed that the temple in Jerusalem had been unclean and dysfunctional since the Zadokite priest had been removed from it. Onias IV purposed to have the

(Acts 8) and Antioch (Acts 12). Both were strongholds of Essene influence because of the treaty agreement between John Hyrcanus and the Seleucid kings of Damascus and Antioch, and because of the faithful service rendered by the followers of John Hyrcanus in military service to the Seleucids. Josephus writes, "The Jews also obtained honors from the kings of Asia, when they became their auxiliaries; for Seleucus Nicator made them citizens of those cities which he built in Asia, and in the Lower Syria, and in the metropolis itself, Antioch."[20]

Those deacons appointed to serve the Hellenistic Essenic Jewish community of Jerusalem left with their flock upon the persecution of Saul to become the leaders of those churches being planted in Cyprus, Phoenicia, and Syria. The rate of exodus from Jerusalem staggered the twelve apostles, as it did the enemy (Saul). Barnabas was sent by the twelve to monitor the progress of the persecuted church in Antioch; Phillip preached to the Ethiopian eunuch and was transported by God straight away to Azotus to lead those fleeing to Phoenicia. However, Saul was sent with letters by the high priest to arrest those fleeing from Jerusalem to Damascus and bring them back to face certain trial, imprisonment, and death. The leadership of the churches emerging from the first Christian dispersion will be covered at length later. This marks the end of the first church in Jerusalem and the beginning of the second.

After the exodus of Essene and Hellenistic Jews to Syria, the apostles made new inroads into the evangelization of the Pharisees, the Sadducees, and the common population of those in Judea, and some were being saved. But Peter was being led out beyond Judea into Lydda, Joppa, Galilee, and Samaria, as he responded to reports that the Jews and Samaritans had believed (Acts 9:31ff.). Peter's travels drew him away from Jerusalem toward the Jews in the Diaspora, as seen in his letter to the παρεπιδήμοις διασπορᾶς, "sojourners of the dispersion." He also acknowledged that his leading was to the Samaritans and the Gentiles as he recounted the events before the Jerusalem council in Acts 15. In addition, at the death of James son of Zebedee, the other apostles were chased away from Jerusalem, including Peter, who had returned from his journey to Samaria and Caesarea: "Tell this to James and the other brethren" and he departed and

---

temple in Leontopolis built in 160 BCE, removing the temple services to the new "clean" temple administered by the Zadokites to serve the Essenes.

20. Josephus *Antiquities* 3.1 (Whiston trans., 251).

went to another place (Acts 12:17). Being in the house of Mary, mother of John Mark, he took Mark with him and ended in Antioch.

By this admission we infer that after James the son of Zebedee was martyred the prominent leadership of the church in Jerusalem went to James the half-brother of Jesus. The church in Jerusalem was about to embark on a new venture. James would lead the church of Jerusalem back to the temple cult. As Bruce writes, "In the early fifty's of the first century James the Just appears as the undisputed leader of the Jerusalem church."[21] This was possible because the make-up of the church was now a newly converted group from among the Pharisees, who were not objects of disdain from the Jewish leadership like the Essenic messianic group, but were more than eager to continue their worship and practice in the accustomed fashion and tradition. The Jewish view of the temple preeminence is clearly observed in the midrash:

> As the navel is set in the centre of the human body,
> so is the land of Israel the navel of the world . . .
> situated in the centre of the world,
> and Jerusalem in the centre of the land of Israel,
> and the sanctuary in the centre of Jerusalem,
> and the holy place in the centre of the sanctuary,
> and the ark in the centre of the holy place,
> and the foundation stone before the holy place, because from it
> the world was founded.[22]

James and other leaders in the newly formed church of Jerusalem had a very difficult time to remove themselves from the Jerusalem worship and the preeminence of the temple and its legal function.

In Acts 15:5, Luke referred to them as the "party of the pharisees" who stood up and said, "it is necessary to circumcise them [the Gentile believers] and to charge them to keep the Law of Moses" (author trans.). This new make-up of the Jerusalem church provisioned the scene that would give the church of Jerusalem standing as a sect of the Jews, but demanded their participation in the temple services, as noticed when James confronted Paul saying, "You see, brother, how many tens of thousands are in the Jews, having believed and all zealots of being ruled of Law" (Acts 21:20 author trans.). This points to James's leading the ἐκκλησία,

21. Bruce, *New Testament History*, 368.
22. *Midrash Tanchuma, Qedoshim.*

the "called out ones," back into the demand of the Law and the temple cult. Those who were "called out" of the Jewish temple worship returned to it. James removed himself from interaction with Gentiles even to the point of not fully embracing Paul and his companions. "But James and his associates compromised themselves in the eyes of the Sanhedrin by receiving Paul."[23] Christ said to the Pharisees, ἠκυρώσατε τὸν λόγον τοῦ θεοῦ διὰ τὴν παράδοσιν, "you have annulled the word of God on account of your tradition" (Matt 15:6). In Jerusalem, therefore, the Word of God took a backseat to the traditions of the Pharisees in the church. The worship through faith that Jesus had generated among the men of Israel by the Spirit excluded any traditional and ceremonial rite. Using the passage in Isaiah, Christ marked his Jewish generation as fulfilling the Scripture that said, "with their lips they honor me, but in vain do they worship me." Christ's call out of the temple cult is also understood in John 4:21–24. Jesus told the Samaritan woman, "believe me, woman, the hour is coming when you will neither worship the Father in this mountain or in Jerusalem . . . when the true worshipers will worship the Father in Spirit and in truth." He was obviously referencing the destruction of the temple in 70 CE, which also indicates the plan and intention of the Lord to stop the temple cult practices.

Paul spent his efforts leading true worshipers, as Christ said, "not in Jerusalem . . . but in Spirit and truth," whereas James led them back to the temple cult. Therefore, there is no ceremony in the Spirit of God by which man can please him or glorify him. In contradiction to the words of Christ and the doctrines of Paul, the Jewish church's behavior precluded any resemblance of grace and promoted a traditional rite for sanctification. James's teaching in Jerusalem brought these three elements to the church in Jerusalem and set in motion the cult of Ebionism.

These heterodox teachings are divisive in nature and built back the dividing wall the God had at length torn down. The first of these teachings is that Paul was an apostate from the Law. This sharply divided the Gentile churches that Paul had established from the Jewish churches. Notice the indictment from James in Acts 21:21 "But they are informed about you, that you are teaching apostasy from Moses to all Jews among the Gentiles, saying [for] them not to be circumcising their children nor to be walking [fig., conducting themselves] [according to] the customs." It is not coinci-

---

23. Bruce, *New Testament History*, 373.

dental that Cerenthus (a known Ebionite) taught in Ephesus that Paul was an apostate from the Law and his writings were to be categorically rejected as blasphemy. He also taught that John the apostle was also to be removed from the church for the same reasons. Some have said that Paul was in agreement and submitted wholly to the ceremony of the temple, and yet the account in Acts 21 is primarily showing the degree of duress that James placed on Paul as he stated that there were tens of thousands of Jewish believers, all zealots for the temple ceremony. But Paul had assurance that his life would be preserved as he pondered the combination of two facts:

1. Agabus had made a prophetic utterance about his visit to Jerusalem.

2. Paul was a Roman citizen, and most Jews in Jerusalem were not.

The second heterodox teaching is that sanctification is by works of law done after baptism. The book of Acts undeniably reveals such anomalies (e.g., having certain hours for prayer, Acts 3:1; offering sacrifices at the temple, Acts 21:23–26). Galatians 3:3 says, "You are so foolish! Having begun in Spirit, are you now being completed (or, perfected) in the flesh?" (author trans.). This context is related to the arguments between Peter and Paul found in Galatians 2 that were being instigated by Jerusalem, and specifically James. Early in the history of the church, a demarcation was set between the Jewish Christian church of Jerusalem and the Greek Christian church of Antioch. Paul exposed the conspiracy when he declared to the churches in Galatia that spies were sent to "spy out" (κατασκοπῆσαι) or also "to lie in wait," declaring that the "false brethren" snuck in (παρεισάκτους) or were smuggled in, which denotes conspiracy on the part of one in leadership. The finger pointed to James, the leader or *episkopos* of Jerusalem, as Paul declared that Peter was brought online by certain ones coming from James. Hence, Peter, who feared the "party of the circumcision," conformed to the instructions and ruling from James in Jerusalem (Gal 2:11–22).

It is also evident that the Jewish believers continued performing the ceremonial works of the Law after the Spirit came. Paul, when raised up as an apostle, was sent by God to the Gentiles with what Paul called "the gospel of the uncircumcision" (Gal 2:7), which excluded every religious ritual known to man, including those rituals that God, through Moses and David, had given to Israel. As Paul understood through Jesus Christ that all of the Law is fulfilled in Jesus Christ, he wrote that "the righteousness of God has been manifested, being witnessed by the Law and the Prophets . . . whom God displayed publicly as propitiation in His blood" (Rom 3:21–25 NASB). By this admission it soon came about that Paul would be known by the natural Jewish Christians as an "apostate from the Law."

This matter of religious ceremony is extremely important because it was on this issue that Paul's gospel for Gentiles differed from James's direction for the Jews. Such evidence supports the activity of James's involvement in the ministry of the temple in Jerusalem. James, a life-long Nazirite[24] was permitted to enter the sanctuary. He wore linen not wool,[25] which distinguished him as performing a priestly function in the temple. The sanctuary here refers to the priestly chamber, or the priestly court containing the altar.[26] This access to the priestly portion of the temple was only assigned for priestly functions upon the approval of Agrippa. Access to the Pinnacle was also denied to the population and reserved for priestly communication. It appears "James wore the linen breeches, the linen coat"[27] (robes) of the priesthood. According to F. F. Bruce, "James's discipleship appears to have begun when he saw Jesus risen from the dead; the evidence of the Gospel tradition is that James and his brothers were not followers of Jesus before that time."[28]

This Gospel evidence comes from John 7 where James and his brothers attempted to set Jesus up by urging him to proceed to Jerusalem for the Feast of Booths. It was clearly known that Jesus's life was in danger in Jerusalem, and John reported that "not even His brothers were believing in Him" (John 7:5). A similar set-up appears in Acts concerning the apostle Paul (Acts 21), when it appears that Paul was urged to enter the temple in order to bring him to harm. The reasoning for the order from James said, "And they are informed of you (Paul), that you teach all the Jews which are among the Gentiles to forsake Moses, saying that they ought not to circumcise their children, neither to walk after the customs" (Acts 21:21

---

24. The lifelong Nazarite vow was reserved for the temple ministry and mostly practiced by the sons of Levi.

25. Bruce, *New Testament History*, 369.

26. Edersheim, *The Temple*, 29–30.

27. Maier, *Eusebius*, 84.

28. Bruce, *New Testament History*, 369.

author trans.). The source of the information is more than likely James, since he was the confirmed bishop of the church and certainly exercised the intention of monarchial order in Jerusalem and spreading through all the churches because of Jerusalem's role in the gospel.

Ultimately, James was martyred in Jerusalem, the temple was destroyed in 70 CE, and the church was scattered in Syria and in Egypt, that is, Damascus and Alexandria, toward the control of the Romans. These Jerusalem-church refugees formed the movement that came to be known by the names Ebionite and Jacobite.

Whereas Rome has claimed the primacy of Peter, Jerusalem and later Damascus claimed the primacy of James. Jacobites and Ebionites alike have issued their doctrines upon the authority of James, these groups finding their support in the regions of Damascus, the Transjordon, and Egypt. According to F. F. Bruce, the safe haven provided to the Jerusalem church in Egypt and the Transjordon "in later generations were main centres of Ebionite Christianity-a form of Jewish Christianity which combined some traditional theology of the Jerusalem church with elements of Samaritan or Essene character."[29] The Jacobite primacy has been taught and was the primary doctrine given through the Gnostic works of the *Gospel of Thomas*, in which we read that the disciples said to Jesus, "We know that you will depart from us. Who is to be our leader?" Jesus said to them, "Wherever you are, you are to go to James the righteous, for whose sake heaven and earth came into being." An early manuscript attributed to the apostles (*Gospel of the Holy Twelve*) also depicts Christ as having said that once he (Christ) was gone, the head of the church would be given to "James the Just," for whom "all heaven and earth were made." Of these manuscripts the *Gospel of Thomas* has been identified with the Gnostic texts and is a part of the Nag Hammadi Library. The *Gospel of the Holy Twelve* has been preserved partially by early church fathers countering the Ebionites, Jacobites, and Gnostics.

THE DOCTRINES OF THE SECOND JERUSALEM CHURCH

Adoptionist Doctrine

Early in the Jerusalem setting lies a misinterpretation by those "reputed as pillars": "Therefore let the entire house of Israel know with certainty that God has made [ἐποίησεν] Him both Lord and Messiah the Jesus whom

29. Ibid., 376.

you crucified" (Acts 2:36 author trans.). The damage done by this statement to the theology of the church in Jerusalem is evident, as Peter stated that Jesus was "made," "created," to be Lord and Christ. This understanding of Jesus as being made or adopted to be both Lord and Christ was a prevalent doctrine among the Jewish Christians and the Ebionites in particular. Certainly Peter's understanding of the role of the Son at this time in his ministry lacked the theological development of Paul and his disciples. The Ebionites referred to "James, the brother God" and distinguished his common parentage with Christ in the natural way. Joseph and Mary were understood in the cult as the biological parents of Jesus the Son of God. The virgin birth was not considered as possible or true. They reasoned that neither the natural laws nor the physical laws of Moses were to be manipulated. The view of the Ebionite (Pharisaic Christian) was that the promised Messiah would be nothing more than a temporal leader, an elevated prophet, a super Lawyer, a reformer of the Law of Moses, and have nothing more than Davidic Jewish roots.

Nevertheless, in the powerless doctrines of the Jacobites and the Ebionites, one could be confused because "a distinction is faintly noticed between the heretics, who confounded the generation of Christ in the common order of nature, and the less guilty schismatics, who revered the virginity of his mother, and excluded the aid of an earthly father."[30]

Jesus Was the Reformer of the Law

James used the nomenclature "perfect law," the finished law (νόμον τέ λειον) the law of liberty, as he states, "But he that looketh into the perfect law, the *law* of liberty, and *so* continueth, being not a hearer that forgetteth but a doer that worketh, this man shall be blessed in his doing. Howbeit if ye fulfill the royal law, according to the Scripture, Thou shalt love thy neighbor as thyself, ye do well" (Jas 1:25 KJV). James's understanding of the finished law would coincide well with the "Jesus reformer of the Law" movement, and according to James it is clear that Paul was instructing Jews and Gentiles alike to disregard the Law, as Moses gave it and Jesus reformed it. It is very curious that James in his Epistle does not mention the three major doctrines of the church: Jesus Christ as being God, the atonement that took place on the cross, and the work of the Holy Spirit in the sanctification of the believer. At the time of the second-, third-,

30. Gibbon, *Decline and Fall,* 5:5.

35

and fourth-century church fathers there was a disregard for the Epistle of James. "Such is the story of James, to whom is ascribed the first of the so-called General Epistles. To be sure, its authenticity is doubted, since not many of the early writers quote it, as is also the case with the epistle of Jude."[31] Yet Eusebius regarded all the fourteen Epistles of Paul as authentic and authoritative but held Hebrews in some question as to its Pauline authorship.[32] Martin Luther called James the epistle of straw and did not include it in his translation of the Greek text. Yet it is not that James should be excluded from the canon, because it serves as a powerful testimony to the history of the early church and the apparent split between Jerusalem and Antioch.

To the Ebionites the Law of Moses was sole authority for the Christian church. Anything changing the physical adherence to it was viewed as blasphemy and as disregard for the Scriptures (Old Testament) and Moses as the emancipator of the Jews. Jesus, according to the Ebionites, was the Reformer of the Law and not the Divine Word, not the One that preexisted as their God. As Gibbon writes,

> A laudable regard for the honor of the first proselyte has coun-
> tenanced the belief, the hope, the wish, that the Ebionites, or at
> least the Nazarenes, were distinguished only by their obstinate
> perseverance in the practice of the Mosaic rites. Their churches
> have disappeared, their books are obliterated: their obscure free-
> dom might allow a latitude of faith, and the softness of their infant
> creed would be variously moulded by the zeal or prudence of three
> hundred years. Yet the most charitable criticism must refuse these
> sectaries any knowledge of the pure and proper divinity of Christ.
> Educated in the school of Jewish prophecy and prejudice, they
> had never been taught to elevate their hopes above a human and
> temporal Messiah.[33]

The death of James marked the end of the second church of Jerusalem. The Ebionite and Jacobite disciples fled Jerusalem for safety to Pella and to Damascus, to Gaza and to Alexandria. Gibbon claimed that the Ebionites ceased to exist; however, that is premature, as the Jehovah's Witnesses and many other Unitarian groups have capitalized on ancient heretical doctrines from them.

31. Maier, *Eusebius*, 84.
32. Ibid., 94.
33. Gibbon, *Decline and Fall*, 1:498–99.

After the 70 CE destruction of the temple, Jewish bishops continued until the bar Kokhba revolt of 115 CE. The church of Jerusalem entered into its third stage, that of a Greek church with Greek patriarchs. Below are the patriarchs of Jerusalem:

Patriarchs of the Jerusalem Church

Jacob/Ya'akov/James the Brother of Jesus	c. 62

Jewish War, 66–73; Jerusalem falls to the Romans; the temple is destroyed, 70

Symeon/Simon I	c. 70–99
Ioustos/Judas/Justus I	99–111
Zakheos/Zakhaios/Zacchaeus Tobias Beniamin/Veniamin/Benjamin I	111–117
John/Ioannis I Matthew/Matthias I Phillip Senekas/Seneca Ioustos/Justus II Levis/Levy/Levi Efrem/Efraim/Ephres Joseph I Judas	117–134

Revolt of Bar Kokhba, destruction of Jerusalem, 132–135

Marcus/Markos/Mark Cassianos/Kassianos/Cassian Pouplios/Publius Maximus I Ioulianos/Julian I Gaios/Gaius I Simmahos/Symmachus Gaios/Gaius II	134–162

Ioulianos/Oialis/Julian II Capion/Kapion/Capito Maximus II Antonios/Antoninus Oualis/Oialis/Valens Dolihianos/Dolichian	162–185
Narkissos/Narcissus II Dios? Germanion? Gordios?	185–211
Alexander	211–249
Mazabanis/Mazabanes	249–260
Imeneos/Ymenaios/Hymenaeus	260–276
Zamvdas/Zambdas/Zabdas	276–283
Ermon/Hermo	283–314
Makarios I	314–333
Maximos III	333–348
Cyrill/Cyrillos I	350–386
John/Ioannis II	386–417
Praulios/Praylios	417–422
Iouvenalios	422–458
Anastasios I	458–478
Martyrios	478–486
Salloustios	486–494
Elias/Helliah I	494–516
John III	516–524
Peter	524–552

3

The Antioch Model

ANTIOCH IN ITS BEGINNINGS

REGARDING THE INCEPTION OF Antioch, Seleucus Nicantor, one of Alexander's generals, built the city early in the third century BCE. The city held strategic value for the Seleucid dynasty, in that it was on the Orontes River which was navigable, and that it was on the trading route from south to north to east to west.[1]

The Seleucid kings made Antioch a showcase city. They built magnificent buildings and adorned Antioch with the luster of precious metals, expensive building materials such as marble, and equipped it with every luxury that would magnify the wealth of the Seleucid Empire. After the Parthian campaign, Antiochus IV provided the city as a colony for faithful Jews who fought on their side. Antiochus granted citizenship, land, preferred tax status.[2] Jews who participated in this colonization effort had been in John Hyrcanus's army.[3] After this Antioch became a refuge for Jews of Hellenistic persuasion who were being persecuted by zealotry in Jerusalem or warfare from the Ptolemy Empire in Egypt. It was incorporated into the Roman Empire in 64 BCE when Pompeii conquered for Rome all of Syria, Palestine, and Idumaea.

1. All overland trade from Egypt was funneled through Antioch.

2. Josephus *Antiquities* 12.3.1.

3. In the *Damascus Document*, the Essenes or party of the Zadokites had ties to the city of Damascus by way of treaty with the Syrian kings and received protection against the "Evil Priest" as he raided from Jerusalem.

HISTORICAL DEMOGRAPHICS OF ANTIOCH

Josephus recorded that at about 130 BCE "many ten thousands of Antiochians"[4] were defending their city from the onslaught of Demetrius, a king of the Seleucids, revealing the fighting strength of the city. The account explains how Jonathan and his Jewish armies were working as mercenaries for Demetrius, and even though the Antiochians raised an army of 40,000 to 50,000 to shake off the ties to Demetrius, they were predisposed to continue the rebellion because their families were in jeopardy in the city. This indicates the population of Antioch at this time to be conservatively 250,000 people.

Josephus further mentioned that in 65 CE the city of Antioch deserved "to be the third [largest, most prominent] city in the habitable earth that was under the Roman Empire,"[5] making Antioch a city of about a half million or more people. By 625 CE Antioch had declined because of the earthquakes of the early seventh century and the Arab incursions. The estimated population was 75,000–100,000. During the revival of the Byzantine naval power of 925 CE, Antioch was recovered by Constantine VII and restored to prominence with a population of over 150,000, and held by the Eastern Empire until 1085.

In 1097 CE the crusaders[6] were "awed by the greatness" and the sight of the walls three miles long and one mile deep. The fortifications were so immense that it was only by treachery that the Muslims acquired the city in 1085 CE when Suleiman ibn Kutulmish captured it, and it was likewise only by treachery that it was taken by the immense crusading army of the Francs and Normans in 1097. Bohemond and his father, Robert Guiscard, had fought the Byzantine Armies of Alexius ten years prior and learned much about the intrigue and treachery required to fight in the Middle East. Early in 1098 Bohemond gained control of the Tower of the Two Sisters by the help of an Armenian Muslim who defected, named Firouz.[7] In 1097 the city was populated by an army of 25,000 Turks needed to control the massive walls, along with their families, servants, and other support persons. The size of Kerboghas's army was 30,000. The crusading

---

4. Josephus *Antiquities* 13.5.3.

5. Josephus *Wars* 3.2.4.

6. Bohemond Son of Robert Guiscard, 1st crusade; Antioch became the Principate of Antioch and was ruled by him.

7. Runciman, *History of the Crusades*, 1:231.

armies at Antioch numbered about 35,000.[8] The account lists the death toll of residents in Antioch at about 150,000, which included women and children. There was not a Turk that survived the siege of Antioch. Rule of thumb would multiply the strength of the combatants by four. The city's population was about one quarter Greeks, about one quarter Jews, and half Turks. Muslims were the only ones who defended the city. Therefore the city's population was about 250,000.[9]

THE TRUE NEW TESTAMENT CHURCH

The New Testament first mentions Antioch in Acts 11. It appears that initially even in Antioch only Jews were invited to participate in the gospel, as it was written, "Then indeed the ones having been scattered because of the affliction [or, persecution], the one having occurred over Stephen, passed through as far as Phoenicia and Cyprus and Antioch, speaking the word to no one except to Jews only" (Acts 11:19).

We discover that the Jews were even withholding the gospel from the Greek-speaking Jews, until Luke recorded that "some of them were male Cypriots and Pyreneans, who having entered into Antioch, began speaking to the Greek-speaking Jews, proclaiming the Gospel of the Lord Jesus" (Acts 11:20). One of these Pyreneans became a leader in the newly formed Gentile church. There were three: Lucas Semen, or Simon of Siren, as he was identified in the Gospels; Mann, who had been a long-time friend of Herod Antipas; and Lucas the physician, who wrote the Gospel of Luke and Acts of the Apostles and became the close companion of Paul. It also appears that this Gentile influence was the first to bring the term "Christian" to bear on the community. For the Jews, this was admittance that Jesus Christ was more than a man, a prophet, and a moralist, but rather the "Holy one from God." Using the Greek word for "Messiah," that is, "Christ," the Gentile believers established their church calling themselves *Christianoi* to distinguish themselves from the Jews who were called "Nazarenes." So, there were two churches in Antioch, one Jewish, and another Gentile.

It is clear that the Essene group upon persecution in Jerusalem was set in motion for evangelism. This comprised the Jewish church of Antioch of which Peter became bishop. Under the leadership and authority of those

8. Ibid., Appendix 2.
9. Ibid., 1:231.

"Hellenistic" deacons appointed by the apostles themselves, the old enemy of the Pharisees, the Essenes, established communities of believers in
other Essene-controlled cities. These were Damascus, Antioch, and Gaff,
according to Acts.

The role of Gentile believers in the Antiochian church was decided
by the council of Jerusalem. Yet it is clear that two groups emerged, one
for the Jews and one for the Gentiles, because it was not in the plans of
that Greek body of believers the Gentiles to be under the subjection of the
Jews in Jerusalem. They were evangelized and led by Hellenistic Jews and
Gentile God-fearers and had no notion that the leaders of the Jerusalem
church were their liege lords. When the church in Jerusalem fell on hard
economic times, several of the Gentile churches led by the apostle Paul
sent love offerings to soften their need. Paul made this clear in his Epistle
to the Corinthians, but it was apparent that the Jerusalem church led by
James saw the gifts as homage.[10]

The writing of the Scriptures was precipitated by events taking place in
churches where the gospel had gone by oral messengers. The Gnostic ideal
was to receive the Old Testament and allegorize it for Gnostic Hellenistic
understanding. Paul controlled the organization to the north (Antioch). In
Pauline literature, literalism responds well to both the allegorical method
of the Gnostics in Alexandria, and the "letteristic" method[11] of the Jews in
Jerusalem. The letteristic character of the Sadducees' interpretation was
applied to the Law only, and it tied up the church in Jerusalem and infil-
trated the Jewish arm of the Antiochian church. By means of edict and
authority James tried to control both Jewish and Gentile denominations
of that church. However, Paul was able to prevent that within the Gentile
congregation by opposing Peter (Gal 2:11–21), and winning him over.
Paul then had a strong ally in Peter at the Jerusalem council in Acts 15.

There are references in 1 Peter that apply more to Gentiles than Jews
(e.g., "once you were not a people"), but Peter could have referred to the
Jewish community of believers that were considered less Jewish, that is,
the "Hellenistic Jews" as compared to the "natural Jews of Judea" in Acts
6. These would have been the ostracized Essenes who had no connec-

10. Bruce, *The Spreading Flame*, 93.

11. Letterism refers to an interpretive method in which every letter is regarded as
necessary to know the true and spiritual meaning of the text, in contrast to a grammatical, literal method of hermeneutics whereby the meanings of words are tied to literary
convention such as ellipsis, typology, symbolism, parallelism, metaphor, etc.

tion to the temple. In fact, they viewed the temple as "unclean" since John Hyrcanus. It is clear in the narrative that the church in Antioch was derived from this group of "Hellenistic Jews."[12] They fled there because of Paul's persecution (he hated the Essenes or "Nazarenes"). Acts also says that they would not preach to the Gentiles (Acts 11:19–22)

It is clear in Paul's Epistle to the Galatians and in Luke's account that in Antioch there were two distinct churches, one Jewish, one Gentile (Gal 2). Paul seems to have ministered to the Gentiles in Antioch, while Peter stayed with the Jews. However, Peter came fully around to Paul's theology of the gospel by Acts 15. This was clearly in opposition to James's statement. But it also appears that Peter was still the bishop over Paul because Paul was a Jew. But Paul started a work with the Gentile believers. Barnabas saw to that by getting Paul from Tarsus. Barnabas knew that Paul, being from Tarsus, was thoroughly familiar by education with Hellenistic philosophies. After all, he had the best of Jewish education and an equally rigorous Hellenistic education; his mentoring professor was Gamaliel, who wrote large portions of the Mishna; he was a natural citizen of Rome by rights of property ownership in Tarsus; and he was of the Herodian family through his father, as he stated, "Greet Herodion, my relative" (Rom 16:11). The term Paul utilized was *syngenē* (συγγένη) literally, "with birth, by birth, blood relative." Peter knew he could not debate with and hold a dialog with the Greek schools of philosophy (Epicureanism, Stoicism, Pythagorianism, Platonism, Aristotelianism, and Sophistry). Paul was equipped to take it all on, but Peter was not.

The passage in Acts 11 introduces the work that began in Antioch. The church there appropriately called out of Barnabas's leadership in the city, and his immediate response was to find Saul or Paul to fill such a great need in the Antioch church. With such a world-class city, a man was needed to minister there with a world-class education, and Barnabas identified Paul as that man.

> And *[the]* hand of *[the]* Lord was with them, and a large number having believed turned to the Lord. Then the word about them was heard in the ears of the assembly, the *[one]* in Jerusalem, and they sent out Barnabas to pass through as far as Antioch, who having arrived and having seen the grace of God, was glad, and began encouraging *[them]* all with purpose of *[or, a resolute]* heart *[fig., with steadfast devotion]* to be continuing with *[fig., remaining loyal*

12. They were the leaders or appointed deacons from Acts 6:3.

to] the Lord, because he was a good man and full of *[the]* Holy
Spirit and of faith. And a considerable crowd was added to the
Lord. Then Barnabas departed for Tarsus to look for Saul. (about
Paul) And having found *[him]*, he brought him to Antioch. So it
happened *[that for]* a whole year they were gathered together with
the assembly and taught a considerable crowd. And the disciples
were first called Christians in Antioch. (Acts 11:21–26)

Earlier in Jerusalem we found Barnabas being raised to deacon, having
been brought forward by the Hellenistic Jews after the contention between
the "natural Jews" and "Hellenistic Jews" in Acts 6. Barnabas was certainly
numbered among the Hellenistic Jews and considered to be one of them,
as the apostles instructed the Hellenistic Jews to "select from among you,
... seven men of good reputation" (Acts 6:3). Nicolas was also chosen, a
"proselyte (gentile convert to Judaism) from Antioch." It was this Nicolas,
according to Eusebius who was the originator of the "Nicolaitans," a so-
called sect that made its appearance Asia Minor and Northern Syria. John
mentioned them in the Apocalypse. They boasted that the author of their
sect was Nicolaus (i.e., Nicholas of Antioch), one of the deacons who, with
Stephen, were appointed by the apostles for the purpose of ministering
to the poor (Acts 6:5). Clement of Alexandria, in the third book of his
Stromata (c. 190 CE), related the following things concerning him:

> They say that he had a beautiful wife, and after the Ascension of the
> Saviour, being accused by the Apostles of jealousy, he led her into
> their midst and gave permission to any one that wished to marry
> her. For they say that this was in accord with that saying of his, that
> one ought to "abuse the flesh." And those that have followed his
> heresy, imitating blindly and foolishly that which was done and
> said, commit fornication without shame. But I understand that
> Nicolaus had to do with no other woman than her to whom he
> was married, and that, so far as his children are concerned, his
> daughters continued in a state of virginity until old age, and his
> son remained undefiled. If this is so, when he brought his wife,
> whom he jealously loved, into the midst of the Apostles, he was
> evidently renouncing his passion; and when he used the expres-
> sion, "to abuse the flesh," he was inculcating self-control in the face
> of those pleasures that are eagerly pursued. For I suppose that, in
> accordance with the command of the Saviour, he did not wish to
> serve two masters, pleasure and the Lord. But they say that [The
> Apostle] Matthias (Acts 1:26) also taught in the same manner that
> we ought to "fight against" and "abuse the flesh," and not give way

to it for the sake of pleasure, but "strengthen the soul by faith and knowledge." So much concerning those who then attempted to pervert the truth, but in less time than it has taken to tell, it became entirely extinct.[13]

Accounts such as these reveal Antioch as a church with mixed groups and alliances, and with diverse and merging Hellenistic philosophical schools.

Raymond Brown and John Meier suggest that Matthew wrote his gospel in Antioch.[14] This establishes a complete picture of the early-second-century theologian Ignatius of Antioch. He combined the organization of Paul and his prescription for dealing with the Gnostic threat with the Jewish flavor of the Gospel of Matthew, acclaiming Christ as the God with us and suffering on the cross in polemic against Docetism, and also with the Logos theology of John.

READING AND INTERPRETATION OF THE WORD

We have stated that the writing of the Scriptures was necessitated by events taking place in the churches where the gospel had gone by oral messengers. The Gnostic foundational philosophy received the Old Testament and allegorized it for Gnostic Hellenistic understanding or dismissed the Old Testament altogether as being the product of a lesser and evil God. To counter the Gnostic influences, Theodore of Mopsuestia, one of the originators of the Antiochene school, taught that the Scripture of the Old and New Testaments was given to meet the needs of man out of historical necessity. Because God intervenes in the physical realm to control the rapaciousness of the sins of men, the Scriptures are tied to and only understood out of that history. However, in contrast, the Alexandrian approach abandoned the methodical and balanced approach of exegesis. The Alexandrian (Philo, Platonist, Origen) view of God's intervention was within God's own spiritual sphere of reference so that the physical history was inconsequential to the writings of the allegory, which reflect only spiritual truth, not historical accuracy.[15]

Paul, controlling the organization to the North (Antioch), wrote in his epistles a literalism that responds well to both the allegorical method

13. Eusebius *Church History* 3.29 (Maier trans., 117).

14. Brown and Meier, *Antioch and Rome*, chap. 1.

15. Wallace-Hadrill, *Christian Antioch*, 52.

of the Gnostics in Alexandria, and the letteristic method of the Jews in Jerusalem. "Antioch, however, was more affected by Jewish thinking, and close affinities between Antiochene and Jewish methods of exegesis have been observed.[16]" The teaching of the Rabbi Paul and the Hillel school of Pharisaic exegesis and its associated rules were "designed to curb speculation."[17] Paul established the Hillel school of interpretation in Antioch and the result allowed Antioch to compete with the school of Philo that was established in Alexandria. Wallace-Hadrill suggests that "Antiochene Christianity became an expression of faith immediately distinguishable from its neighbors" to the north and south, bringing Antioch into prolonged conflict with the great ecclesiastical centers of Constantinople and Alexandria."[18] However, this is only true in regard to Alexandria and Jerusalem, not Constantinople,[19] which was not a center of Christianity until 325, and the Antiochian school provided a long line of patristic fathers in Constantinople who agreed with the patriarchs of Antioch. These included Nestorius and John Chrysostom.

In evaluating any connection between Antiochian theology and the Logos theology of Tertullian, the proposal of some contact between the early Christians of Antioch and the early Christians of Carthage is conjecture. Nevertheless, it is not out of the question in light of the spread of Christianity throughout the Mediterranean in the first and second centuries being an equally amazing and quick process. The infrastructure of the Roman system was strong and established. The Roman rubric for transporting a legion (approximately 10,000 fighting troops, not counting support) from one end of the empire to the other was a month (30 days). There was also a strong commercial and military connection between Carthage and Gaul. This was established early during the Punic wars with the onslaught of Hannibal and his massive army in the third century BCE. The early church connection seems more feasible in light of Paul's ministry to Gaul and Spain and the churches he had likely established in the region. Any church that was established by Paul would have

---

16. Ibid., 30.

17. Ibid., 30.

18. Ibid., 14.

19. Wallace-Hadrill includes Constantinople as an established center of Christianity, but that is not so until after Constantine. This either reveals that the author is inclined to agree with the academics that promote Christianity as a Constantinian invention or that he has become reckless with his chronology.

propagated Pauline interpretative methodology as established at Antioch on the Orontes River.

The bulk of the New Testament was written by the apostle Paul in response to questions arising in the churches that he had planted in the north. Because the apostle Paul took a literal grammatical approach to the Old Testament and wrote in a literal and specific style, the approach to Old Testament hermeneutics from the school of Antioch followed the illustration given by Paul in his Epistles. Where allegory was to be applied he clearly stated that in his text in Galatians 4:21–31. Therefore, there is no epistle written directly to the Alexandrians, to the Damascenes, to the Pellites.

THE ANTIOCHIAN SCHOOL OF INTERPRETATION

Pauline authority permeated the Antiochian church. The Antiochian theologians pushed to abandon the stiff letteral interpretation of the Old Testament of the Sadducees and the allegorical method of the Alexandrians. They viewed the balance of a literal interpretation of grammar and history to be paramount to the understanding of the Old Testament, and they saw the clearness of the writings of Paul as bringing the proper interpretation of Scriptures to light. Opposing Origen, Lucian and other theologians from Syria, the school instructed the church in the typological connection between the Old and New Testaments, and made the school of interpretation at Antioch into a leading biblical institute. But even at an early date the Antiochian bishopric was instrumental in establishing orthodoxy. One such bishop and contemporary of John the apostle was Ignatius. In about 96 CE during the Domitian persecution, Ignatius of Antioch wrote to the Ephesians, "Jesus Christ the inseparable one, our life, is the mind of the father."[20] The context was the support of the ordained bishop of Ephesus, Onesiphorus. The message however is clear. Ignatius understood the implications of the Logos theology of John and the teaching of Paul on the preexistence of the Son and the sameness of nature and being that the Son has with the Father.

Antioch and Alexandria were the emerging schools of biblical inter-pretation starting in the second century. Antioch was the school of literal biblical interpretation, while Alexandria was the school of allegorical bib-

20. Ignatius *To the Ephesians* 3:2 (author's translation). Ἰήσουη Χρίστουη, τό ἀδι-ακρίτου ἡμῶν ζήν, τοῦ πατρούη ἡ γνώμη.

lical interpretation. The former is tied to the grammar, while the latter is tied to higher, "spiritualization." The former has rules and skills, which make it a science and an art. The latter has imagination, which makes it fantasy. Not all the Antiochene theologians were orthodox, but by using a literal grammatical approach to studying the Bible they were bound to keep the faith apostolic. The table on page 49 compares the differences between the two competing schools of biblical interpretation.[21]

In Antioch, as in the entire East, with time, Orthodoxy became more detailed and specific. But from the beginning there were certain doctrines that were primary to the faith. These were the resurrection of the body, the Deity of Jesus Christ, the preexistence of Christ, monotheism, and the forgiveness of sins by the work of Christ, salvation through faith and not works. These comprised the heart of Pauline theology. With time and the absence of apostolic protection from heresies, orthodoxy not only dealt with the great doctrines of the faith, but also needed a comprehensive method of translation, interpretation, and systematization to deal with the plethora of cult movements that emerged from the incorporation of Hellenistic and Jewish philosophical schools. These were promoted by overt and covert actions on the part of Jews responding negatively to the gospel, and Gentiles responding negatively to the Christians as being a mere sect of Judaism. The heretical cults found their promoters in prophets, scholars, teachers and even secular leaders who were driven by the goal of destroying the newfound "paganism."[22]

Antioch established a highly critical exegetical school that intricately connected the grammatical interpretation of the Scriptures and the historical accounts to the theology of its school. In opposition to this milieu, the Latin West (excepting Carthage, led by Tertullian and Augustine) used

---

21. *Protestant Biblical Interpretation* by Bernard Ramm is a good source for understanding the differences between Antioch and Alexandria, which are presented very well in his section "Historical Schools." Two good words to know are *exegesis* and *isogesis*. *Exegesis* (found at the Antiochian school) means to draw out from its source or beginning or look to see what is written and understanding (drawing out) what it means. *Isogesis* (found at the Alexandrian school) means to put something into its source or beginning, which means that I go to the Scripture and put into it my own thoughts so that I make it say what I want it to say.

22. The Romans viewed the "Christians" as a cult of the Jews in the first century, while in the second century the empire's authorities understood that Christianity was not connected to Judaism, therefore it must be a new pagan religion because it did not recognize the legally recognized gods.

Schools of Biblical Interpretation

	Alexandrian School	Antiochene School
Author/ Disciples:	Plato, Philo, Clement, Origen	Hillel, Paul, Theodore, Ignatius, Lucius
Old Testament:	Shadow of things theological Body or flesh of the Scripture	Historical event of theological doctrine
New Testament:	Image of things theological Soul of the Scripture	Fulfilled history of theological doctrine
The Realm of Heaven:	Spiritual reality of things theological Spirit of the Scripture	Glorified and culminated history of theological doctrine
Methodology:	Allegorical method	Literal method
	Symbolic foundation to be understood as an extended metaphor of heavenly reality Isogesis	Historical foundation to be understood literally and typologically Exegesis
Philosophy:	Dualism	Realism and pragmatism
Historical Trinitarian Doctrinal position:	Trinity: Homoiousian	Trinity: Homoousian
	Promotes tri-theism, *tritoi theoi*	Promotes mono-theism within the triunity of the one God
Genesis:	Waters above the firmament are spiritual powers	Waters are waters; Porphyry calls the method of Origen "pretentious obscurity."

the Alexandrian method of allegory to simplify and codify theology according to a Western Latin scheme.

This process of Western codification set the stage for misinterpretation of the Greek texts, the Latinization, and allegorization of the Scriptures. We find this confusion even in Greek grammars on the market today. This false Latinization of hermeneutics and translations of the Bible is pointed out by grammarians such as A. T. Robertson, for instance: "Most of the older Greek grammars were made by men who knew Latin better than Greek. Even today the study of Greek tenses is hampered by the standpoint of Latin idioms which developed under very different conditions. This is true of school grammars in particular, whereas Latin has had no influence on the Greek tenses by the time of koine"[23] Also in my own work, "In English and Latin grammars there is no participle as the Attic understands it, therefore the Latin Vulgate translates the koine Greek mood (participle) as an imperative, or an indicative, or a subjunctive. It is most common to translate the second person participle as an imperative and the third person participle as an indicative."[24] Problems arise in the translation of tenses in non-indicative-mood verbs the Latin makes no distinction of time, where the Greek does. Prepositions usually lose their detail of position and direction because of problems within the Latin Vulgate. This is understood in two camps of grammarians, the Cambridge approach to Greek vs. the Oxford approach to Greek.

The influence of Latin allegorical methodology on the Western church is most visible when reading the Ante-Nicaean church fathers in Greek. We note that the Greek New Testament is not a "translation" because the autographs of the New Testament were written in Greek. But the Greek New Testament cannot be influenced by translating from one language to another. That makes all translations only as good as the skills and the integrity of the translators. Since the Eastern churches' native tongue was Greek, they were not influenced by such a translation process. It should be noted here that Erasmus identified the problem in the sixteenth century, but he was censored by the Vatican under threat of excommunication.

---

23. Robertson, *A Greek Grammar*, 822.
24. Thompson, "Limited Word Translation," 218.

THE NEW TESTAMENT CANON

In Antioch, the New Testament (the twenty-seven books comprising the canon) found its adherers though a very different process than did the Old Testament. The Antiochian church was the proving ground for Christian mysticism being imported from Parthia, Persia, Media, and Elam. Spurious writings came from the East with heretical teachers and doctrines promoting food laws, ascetic lifestyles, and experiential theology. Unlike the Old Testament preserved as canon, the New Testament had no priesthood, no synagogue system, and no mishnah to enable the Christians to properly interpret the texts. Antioch was stuck between two groups, the Jews, who had stiff letterism imposed on the Torah by the high Priesthood, and the Alexandrian allegorical camp promoted by the Hellenistic Jew Philo.

While Jerusalem still remained the cultural and hermeneutical school of Old Testament studies for the Jews until 115 CE, the Christians in Alexandria sought to establish their difference from Judaism and therefore thought it necessary to distinguish Old Testament hermeneutics from the physical and fleshly Jewish rabbinic traditions. In Antioch the allegorical methodology collided with Persian mysticism. Because of the various heretical churches and their pseudepigraphal writings, Christians pondered which books they should teach, which they would die for, and what books taught the truth. Cults produced their own sets of books. Marcion in the second century CE authorized only Luke and ten of Paul's Epistles that were void of any Old Testament reference and critical of Jewish society, forcing the orthodox church to formally recognize writings that were authentic, authoritative, and connected to eyewitnesses of Jesus's earthly ministry.

The process of canonization for the New Testament is known from the many secondary documents that were circulating in private libraries. However, the process can be likened to that of the Old Testament in that canonization happened over periods of time as the community of God's people became familiar with the different books and got copies of them. Most copies were partial texts of New Testament documents owned and copied by private citizens for private use. However, we cannot assume that canons of Scripture were popping up all over with varying books because the apostolic and post-apostolic churches were unified in their use of the Old Testament Scriptures and of the New Testament writings that were accepted and known as authentically apostolic. By the time of Nicaea, Eusebius tells us that all the writings currently accepted as the "Word of God" were unanimously revered in all the churches except five (James, Jude, 2 Peter, 2 John, 3 John).[25] Only the heretical churches (Ebionite, Jacobite, and Gnostic) had accepted pseudepigrapha and other irrelevant documents. For example, some books were written to certain places such as Rome (Romans) or even to individuals (Gaius in 3 John). It would take a good amount of time before that document circled back to Antioch, Jerusalem, and the other Christian communities. Those books that were questioned were often excluded from one center of the church or another. We note in Colossians 4:16 the description of how the letter was to be distributed: "And when this letter is read among you, *have it also read in the church of the Laodiceans; and you, for your part read my letter that is coming from Laodicea.*" It appears that Paul was fairly methodical about his writings, as Peter ascribes and acknowledges Paul's Epistles as "Scripture" and equal in authority to the Old Testament. This may be evidence that all of Paul's writings were sent in copy back to his home church of Antioch, as Peter was their first bishop according to the local church histories.

"Over time, the twenty-seven different documents of the New Testament traveled about and ended up in different Christian churches or Christian centers. Each main Christian center began their own collection of these New Testament Scriptures (i.e., manuscripts) by making their copies."[26] Some books never got to another center during this period. This produced some question about whether the book was authentic. Most books, however, "were easily accepted," because the books that became quickly and widely distributed to those who saw the eyewitnesses of the Lord's ministry could authenticate the message, the style, and even the handwriting of the originals. Notice Paul's comment to the believers receiving his Epistle indicating that his handwriting was distinct and that they knew it: "The greeting by the hand of me, Paul" (Col 4:18). The authenticity of other writings was debated because they were less known, not attested, and contradicted the gospel. However, twenty of the twenty-

25. Maier, *Eusebius*, 115.
26. Bucknell, "Origins of the Bible."

seven books were clearly accepted by 180 CE. Athanasius, as the bishop of Alexandria, listed the twenty-seven books in 367 CE. The councils of Hippo (393) and Carthage clearly accepted as Holy Scripture and canonized the 27 books known to Protestants as the New Testament, and the Chalcedon Council in 451 CE merely affirmed what had already been clearly established.[27]

ORGANIZATIONAL CHANGES TO MEET THE NEED

In Antioch, the leadership was split for ministry to the differing groups. Peter ministered to the Jews, while Barnabas and Lucius Simon (Simon of Cyrene) ministered to the Hellenistic Jews, and Luke ministered to the Gentiles. The early segregation of church groups and church leadership was always a product of Jerusalem, who had not torn down the wall between Jew and Gentile. Jerusalem always held the position that the entire Gentile church owed allegiance and tribute to the Jerusalem church and its leaders. Their position was clear in regard to the free will offering given to them by Antioch and other churches, including Corinth. Jerusalem held that such offering was due them by divine right. However, Paul continued to encourage the Gentiles to show love to the Jews in Jerusalem by their kindness and brotherly concern for them with such free-will gifts.[28]

It is not known whether the *episkopos* office was set up first in Antioch or Ephesus, as the Scripture might indicate that the *episkopos* office had earlier roots than Paul's letter to Timothy. Paul suggested to Timothy to set up the episcopal administration in Ephesus to prevent "some men from teaching strange doctrines" in the church that Paul had founded. It could be argued from Paul's letter that he was confident in that form of government because it had already succeeded in Antioch. By the time of the *Church History* of Eusebius of Caesarea (330), the apostolic succession of its bishopric was well established.

THE GOVERNMENT AND RULE OF JULIAN THE APOSTATE

Having established his palace in Antioch, Julian, wishing to strike a blow against the "Galileans" began a two-pronged pogrom against the church. First, he removed the Antiochene church lands once controlled by the pagan cults and restored them for the worship of those deities. Secondly,

27. Ibid.

28. Bruce, *Advance of Christianity*, 93.

Lucifer and Eusebius were recalled from banishment, hoping that such a machination would put the church in disorder by releasing the orthodox Homoousian bishops, and establishing a dual bishopric where the Homoiousian bishops had sole power. He intended that open civil war would break out in those churches. He had good reason to believe his plan would have success, as Socrates Scholasticus claims, "he [Lucifer] himself went to Antioch, where he found the church in great disorder, the people not being agreed among themselves."[29] The plan seemed to be working to perfection, when Lucifer consecrated Paulinus in Antioch as bishop. However, reestablishing the pagan rites in Antioch only unified the two bickering theologies against the common and greater foe. Julian became a laughing stock in Antioch, and prayers and entreaties began in the church to remove Julian from power.[30] A particularly graphic description is given of Julian in the writings of Socrates Scholasticus,

> For it seemed to me that no good was portended by a neck seldom steady, the frequent shrugging of shoulders, an eye scowling and always in motion, together with a frenzied aspect; a gait irregular and tottering, a nose breathing only contempt and insult, with ridiculous contortions of countenance expressive of the same thing; immoderate and very loud laughter, nods as it were of assent, and drawings back of the head as if in denial, without any visible cause; speech with hesitancy and interrupted by his breathing; disorderly and senseless questions, answers no better, all jumbled together without the least consistency or method.[31]

His physical appearance and demeanor were so horrendous to the Antiochians that songs were sung about Julian in public, and his anger burned against Antioch. There was no mutual admiration between the emperor and the city of Antioch, for as much hated as Julian had become, the city was equally loathed by Julian.

Persia invaded Asia Minor and the city of Nisibis just East of Edessa came under siege. Having been sent an urgent request for help, Julian returned his reply. He chastened them for not reestablishing the pagan temples, for as Sozomen wrote, "when the inhabitants of Nisibis sent to implore his aid against the Persians, he [Julian] refused to assist them because they were wholly Christianized, and would neither reopen their

29. Socrates Scholasticus, *Church History*, 80.
30. Ibid., 85.
31. Ibid., 92.

temples nor resort to the sacred places."[32] His reply stated sharply that he would not lift a finger until they "had returned to paganism."

By the time Julian marched on his Persian campaign, the collective prayers of the church of Antioch were focused on his demise. Even his pagan counselors had received oracles about the tragedy facing Julian and warned him not to proceed. The Persian campaign in its early stages was wildly successful, bringing Julian to the gates of the Persian capital Ctesiphon. But a bigger Persian army was marching to its aid. Julian single-mindedly moved forward and circumstances became dire, prompting his retreat, which brought the onslaught of jackals at the back-peddling Roman legions. In the last battle, Julian was killed and all was lost. Jovian, his general and an orthodox Christian, sued for a treaty, and led the long retreat back to Constantinople.

The unity of the Homoousians and Homoiousians in Antioch only lasted while Julian remained alive. Immediately upon the death of Julian the groups sought to win the affection of Jovian, the next emperor. Even as Jovian trudged with his army back from the defeat at Ctesiphon the divided Christian parties were manuevering for position. When Jovian entered Antioch, even Macedonians and Acacians met and affirmed their faith in the Nicene orthodoxy. These two groups had plans to be sure, since Melitius was in high esteem with Jovian.[33] Their petition raised before Jovian was "expell from all churches" "all those who asserted the Son to be unlike the Father."[34] Jovian's response ended for a time the posturing and dissention between the groups. He remarked, "I abominate contentiousness; but I love and honor those who exert themselves to promote unanimity!"[35]

After Jovian returned to Constantinople the Homoousians, the Homoiousians, and the Homoians descended upon Jovian a second time to convince him that protection from each other's oppositional doctrines also "meant power against their opponents."[36] Such splits brought about new groups or cults of Christians. The mutual loathing reemerged only to bring about the great fifth-century debates, and sparked a raft of general

---

32. Sozomen *Ecclesiasticus* 5.3.

33. Socrates Scholasticus, *Church History*, 94.

34. Ibid.

35. Ibid.

36. Ibid.

church councils. One such cult that had been influenced by Julian and had possibly renounced Christianity during Julian's reign and reemerged into Christian churches after his death was the Messalians.

The Messalians were an ascetic group of Christians believing that the devil works his wiles among the baptized. This group had its beginnings in paganism and syncretically incorporated the paganism and polytheism of Julian into the Christian vocabulary. Its early non-Christian sect was said to have admitted a plurality of gods, "but to have worshipped only one, the Almighty (*Pantokrator*)."[37] Constant prayer directed to the Holy Spirit would enable the Holy Spirit to independently answer, because he is an independent agent and indeed another God. Later, this group influenced the Bogamils of Bulgaria. Groups such as these changed their names and genealogies of teachers to confound the ruling of Nicaea.

Each cult group incorporated the *tritoi theoi*, "three Gods," of Origen, the intense allegorism of the Scriptures, and the experiences of mysticism and asceticism as rationale for their so-called truth to disturb the church in Antioch. The intensity in which these cults found a voice at Antioch was staggering. Antioch became the crossroads for every wind of doctrine, and every heresy sought acceptance in Antioch. Antioch now emerged as a proving ground for new doctrines and for new explanations of old heretical ones.

After the death of Jovian, Valentinian was elevated to the purple. Valentinian was orthodox but exercised tolerance toward both positions. He preferred the throne of the West and decided to share the crown with his brother Valens, who was placed to rule in the East. It appears that Valentinian preferred the region of the empire that sought less debate. Milan held the administrative government of the West, while Rome the ecclesiastical rule, and was less complex, simpler, and certainly less educated.

Valens, having received the East, was militantly Arian and began a pogrom of persecution against the Homoousian bishops and churches. A particularly hostile persecution was raised in Antioch by Valens. Antioch had a history of bad blood with emperors, and Valens was no exception. According to Socrates,

> the Emperor Valens, little affected by the calamities resulting from the famine, went to Antioch in Syria, and during his residence

37. Arendzen, "Messalians," 212.

there cruelly persecuted such as would not embrace Arianism. For not content with ejecting out of almost all the churches of the East those who maintained the "homoousian" opinion, he inflicted on them various punishments besides. He destroyed a greater number even than before, delivering them up to many different kinds of death, but especially drowning in the river [Orontes].[38]

Such severe persecution on the part of the Arian emperor brought greater turmoil to the city of Antioch. Having orthodoxy removed by force, the church in Antioch struggled in exile and in secrecy. Valens strove to make the unity in the East an Arian one, and the Arians were only too pleased to destroy the Homoousian churches and its adherents. From this time on, the two groups would struggle for the superior position. When the Homoiousians would take the authority, the Homoousians would meet in secrecy. When the Homoousians would take the authority, the Homoiousians would meet in secrecy or raise riots to get the attention of the emperor.

THE FIFTH-CENTURY DEBATES

"The council of Nicaea had treated *hypostaseis* and *ousia* as interchangeable terms, and this had caused some considerable confusion, especially in the West, since it was not clear when people were speaking of three persons and when they were speaking of three godheads."[39] When Tertullian had made his statement concerning the three *personae* the term was clearly not used to depict person or being. Because Tertullian was a jurist in the Roman legal system, his reference was the legal definition: *personae*, as Tertullian used it, referred to the "mask," the role, the appearance, the face. By redefining the term in the Latin West, confusion emerged in the East, sparking another onslaught of debates between the Homoousians and the Homoiousians. These debates were exacerbated in Antioch, where two opposing factions battled for doctrinal standing. This redefinition of term allowed *hypostaseis* to be the Greek translation of the Latin *personae* instead of *prosōpon* (face). Those who held to the Nicene doctrine were Paulinas and Evagrius. Those who held to the Homoiousian position were Melitius, Flavian and Gregory of Nyssa, one of the Cappadocian fathers. While the Homoousians held the biblical orthodox position, the

---

38. Socrates Scholasticus, *Church History*, 104.
39. Davidson, *A Public Faith*, 79.

Homoiousians held the seat of ecclesiastic power in Antioch, making them the historical orthodox party. But in debate, which was allowed in the East and not in the West, the orthodoxy of the Homoousians could become confused. It was imperative that the roles of the Father and that of the Son not become confused and the doctrine devolve into Sabellianism.

The danger lay in *hypostaseis* being separated from *ousias*. This new doctrine brought about a tritheism that was mixed with orthodox terms that were defined in an Arian way.[40] Gregory of Nyssa forwarded an example of *hypostaseis* as being like Peter, James, and John, which truly reflected the confusion that emerged from the misuse of the term. Yet Gregory wrote a treatment called "To Abladius: On Why There Are Not Three Gods." His treatment inadequately explained that the term *Theos* "can only be used in the singular and that God is inherently incomposite."[41] The three *hypostaseis*, he states, "share in a unity of will, purpose, and power,"[42] in other words, by some sort of agreement. Later the West used this argument to add superfluous text to 1 John 5:8: "in heaven, the Father, the Word, and the Holy Spirit, and these three are one (in agreement)." The conflict that occurred in Antioch came in the years after Nicaea when the Homoousian theologians tried to further tie in the oneness of the one God of the Scriptures in Homoiousian or Homoian settings. The product of the later councils brought about an Arian compromise and an anathematization of many orthodox bishops who sought to answer all the small doctrinal inconsistencies designed to dilute orthodoxy.

The death of the orthodox bishop Paulinus sent a tremor felt in all of Syria and Asia Minor. Those who were ministered to by Paulinus refused the next appointee, Flavian. They brought before them Evagrius, ordaining him to their own party. The schism was short lived, because Evagrius was very old, and lived only a short time. Even so, the Evagrius party kept meeting separately, and had no bishop. "Flavian 'left no stone unturned,' as the phrase is, to bring these also under his control."[43] He soon gained control of the factions by wooing and winning over Theophilus, who was bishop of Alexandria. Then by making alliance with Theophilus, he also won the trust of Damasus, bishop of Rome. Socrates records,

---

40. Ibid., 91.

41. Gregory of Nyssa, *On Why There Are Not Three Gods.*

42. Ibid.

43. Socrates Scholasticus, *Church History*, 125.

both these had been greatly displeased with Flavian, as well for the perjury of which he had been guilty, as for the schism he had occasioned among the previously united people. Theophilus therefore being pacified, sent Isidore a presbyter to Rome, and thus reconciled Damasus, who was still offended; representing to him the propriety of overlooking Flavian's past misconduct, for the sake of producing concord among the people. Communion being in this way restored to Flavian, the people of Antioch were in the course of a little while induced to acquiesce in the union secured. Such was the conclusion of this affair at Antioch. But the Arians of that city being ejected from the churches, were accustomed to hold their meetings in the suburbs."[44]

ORTHODOX NICENE BISHOPS

The fifth century saw further departures from the Nicene position, as Homoousians tried to explain the unity and sameness of the persons of the Trinity by overemphasizing or detracting from Christ's humanity. These over reactive-doctrines became points of contention with the Christology that would emerge from Nicaea and the doctrines pertaining to the atonement. The strong tradition of the school of Antioch, and the Pauline understanding of Christ made the history of Antioch volatile. To oppose a nonbiblical view and to reestablish Nicene orthodoxy after its violent overthrows, kept the city of Antioch in turmoil after Constantine died.

These fifth-century debates provided a milieu that I describe as cult-orthodoxy. The detail of the debates between the Homoousians and the Homoiousians became so particular and intense that those who participated trapped themselves into the language that they employed to maintain Nicene orthodoxy, or to defeat Arianism, or to incorporate Arianism. Antioch became embroiled into the doctrine of the dual nature of Christ, while the Arian Alexandrian party took opportunity at the death of Athanasius to redesign Arianism through those similar debates. Some doctrinal camps can be observed to be Arian compromises (Monophysitism, Novationism, Monothelitism), others as articulate and definitive camps to prevent the spread of destructive secondary teachings (Nestorianism). By the rhetoric that they used to put an end to Arianism or to compromise with it, they entrapped themselves into cult-orthodoxy.

44. Ibid., 126.

That is not to say that any doctrine of Arianism should be considered orthodox from a biblical perspective, but it is clear that most of the church in the West and the East after these debates establish semi-Arianism as the historical orthodoxy of the day. We can explain cult-orthodoxy two ways:

1. The orthodoxy of Nicaea was being eroded by continued bombardment of Arian infiltration, which made the orthodoxy depart from an exegetical biblical systematic theology to an isogetical experiential and historical orthodoxy.

2. Those who maintained the Nicene theology of 325 became overpowered by Arian compromise and aggressive overt dissention and they fled into the shadows and became secretive, deposed, and a cult to the Homoian and Homoiousian Christians.

Yet they still held to Nicene orthodoxy. Such were men like Nestorius, who became the patriarch of Constantinople and lost his position at the hands of Cyril of Alexandria and John of Antioch, who also opposed Cyril but was deposed and replaced by his nephew Domnus, who appointed Irenaeus, a known Nestorian, to the Bishopric of Tyre. The war between Cyril and Nestorius divided the East into two main camps of theology and numerous subgroups of radicals and moderates. The rest of the fifth, sixth, and seventh centuries were driven by the strife of the meanness perpetuated by Cyril and the abuse endured by Nestorius. Cyril's Monophysitic moderation clouded the issue and created a group of moderate Chalcedonians who despised Constantinople and Antioch, and a radical Monophysitic church in Egypt willing to employ violence as a means to an end. The Byzantine emperors of those centuries each worked feverishly to bring about a theological unity that was much needed to stem the tide of enemies abroad and within. The intensity of the struggle created a chasm of unapproachable distance so that, "by the end of the seventh century, there was plainly very little prospect of reconciling the friends and foes of Chalcedon."[45] If the objective of Chalcedon was to promote unity in the catholic church it was an abject failure. The next series of theological debates centered on the christological concerns about the union or division of the two natures of Christ after the incarnation.

45. Davidson, *A Public Faith*, 237.

Much of the debate pitted Nestorius against Cyril in a manner that elevated speculation as to what Nestorius's heresies were. All manner of propaganda was used to distort the words of Nestorius and kept condemning him. His writings, having been ordered to be burned, were not allowed to defend him even after his death. He was not exonerated in name at Chalcedon, but his doctrines were. As Nestorius wrote in his defense, "Why then dost thou calumniate me, saying 'He has posed this inquiry', and call me an inventor of novelties and a cause of disturbance and war, me who have posed absolutely no such inquiry but, to be sure, found it in Antioch? And there I taught and spoke concerning these things and no man blamed me, and I supposed that this dogma had long been repudiated"[46] Nestorius illuminates the actions taken against him by Cyril when he writes,

> Wickedly you have separated off a party against me and there was not any one to contend; on my account you have obtained by [your] authority the documents from a number of bishops, every one [of whom] was as one dumb and deaf. You have assembled a company of monks and of those who are named bishops for the chastisement and disturbance of the church, and there is none of the chiefs who has hindered [it] that it might be prevented. An assembly such as this which was sent, came and appeared as a guard against me in the Imperial Palace. You have all the support of the Empire, whereas I [have] only the name of the Emperor, not [indeed] to overpower [you] nor to guard [me] nor for my own help, but rather as if to [ensure] my obedience. Because indeed I made no use of the support of the church nor of the support of the chief men nor of the support of the Empire, I am come to this extremity. But I, who had the chief men and the Emperor and the episcopate of Constantinople, I, who had been long-suffering unto heretics, was harassed by thee so as to be driven out; and thou wast bishop of Alexandria and thou didst get hold of the church of Constantinople—a thing which the bishop of no other city whatsoever would have suffered, though one wished to judge him in judgement and not with violence. But I have endured all things while making use of persuasion and not of violence to persuade the ignorant; and I looked for helpers, not for those who contend in fight and cannot be persuaded.[47]

46. Nestorius *Bazaar of Heracleides* 1.3.
47. Ibid.

Nestorius, utilizing the Scripture, put together an apologetic for his position that described the incarnation as a σχῆμα, "form, appearance."[48] After all of the criticism of the Nicene Creed by the Homoiousian and Homoian parties, he felt that his position was better served by utilizing terms that were used by the apostle Paul in the same light. Unfortunately, the bishops of the time were not listening, according to the Western traditions.

In 449 Theodosius II feared that a resurgence of Nestorianism was at hand and deposed Domnus and his appointed bishop by calling together the second council of Ephesus. Theodosius's concerns were founded not only on Domnus's appointment of Irenaeus, but also on Domnus's defense of Ibas, bishop of Edessa, against charges of teaching Nestorian doctrines and his summoning of a council at Antioch in 448, which decided in favor of Ibas and deposed his accusers. Domnus's sentence of 449 CE at the second council of Ephesus was revoked by Flavian, patriarch of Constantinople, but was reconfirmed by three episcopal leaders to whom Flavian and the emperor Theodosius had given authority over the case.

Antioch always remained beyond the complete control of the Muslims. From the onslaught of Islam in the early to middle seventh century, Antioch rarely fell under complete Islamic control. Because of its importance to the Byzantine Empire, Constantinople and the emperors were always quick to wrest it from the Turks if they penetrated its defenses. Even when it was lost to Malik Shah after Constantinople's defeat at Manzikert, Antioch held out for over twenty years until 1089 when the city came to an agreement with the Turks. From that time, Alexius saw that Antioch would play a major role in the restoration of Byzantine strength and stability, but unfortunately he had to spend much of his resources battling the Normans, particularly Robert Guisgard and his son Bohemond, who viewed Constantinople as an apple to be plucked from the Greeks since their defeat at Manzikert.

Before the declaration of crusade by Pope Urban II in 1096, the West viewed the East with theological disgust. It is more than certain that Urban discussed such things with the princes who answered the call of the cross, because all the princes except Raymond of Toulouse referred to the Byzantines as heretics. It was not that the East had changed their orthodox position. The Greeks and especially the Antiochian patris

48. Phil 2:7–8: καὶ σχήματι εὑρεθεὶς ὡς ἄνθρωπος ἐταπείνωσεν ἑαυτὸν γενό μενος ὑπήκοος μέχρι θανάτου, θανάτου δὲ σταυροῦ.

remained Nicene, defending the Creed in its early form. Antioch and Constantinople even used the anathemas as a rule to distinguish itself from all who would pervert it.

At the first crusade, Antioch remained the center for orthodoxy in Asia Minor and Syria, however small that influence was in a Muslim-held land, until Bohemand deposed the orthodox patriarch for a Latin imposter in 1098. The orthodox patriarch held the theological scepter, but Bohemond made himself the primary enemy of Nicene orthodoxy, as Runciman writes, "in Antioch, thanks to Bohemond, the schism between the Churches was now made definite."[49]

By 1159, life for those who held the Antiochene orthodoxy was abysmal at best. A letter from the patriarch of Antioch to Louis VII reads:

> The deaths of the Christians are frequent and the captures which we see daily. Moreover, the wasting away of the church in the East afflicts with ineradicable grief to us who, tortured internally even to our destruction, are dying while living in anguish of soul, and, leading a life more bitter than death, as a culmination of our miseries, are wholly unable to die. Nor is there anyone who turns his heart towards us and out of pity directs his hand to aid us. But not to protract our words, the few Christians who are here cry out to you, together with us, and implore your clemency, which with God's assistance is sufficient to liberate us and the church of God in the East.[50]

From that time on the orthodox patriarch of Antioch has been in exile. But this time period lies outside the scope of this book. Below is a table of patriarchs ruling from Antioch.

Patriarchs of Antioch

St. Peter the Apostle	37/45–53
Euodius	c. 53–c. 68
St. Ignatius	c. 68–107
Hero I	107–c. 127
Cornelius	c. 127–c. 154

49. Runciman, *History of the Crusades*, 1:321.

50. Letter from Aymeric, patriarch of Antioch, to Louis VII of France, 1164.

Eros/Heros II	c. 154–c. 169
Theophilus	c. 169–182
Maximus I/Maximianus	182–191
Serapion	191–211/212
Ascelpiades/Aslipiades	211/212–218/220
Philetus	220–231
Zebinnus/Zebinus/Zenobius	231–237
St. Babylas	237–253
Fabius	253–256
Demetrius/Demetrian	256–260
Amphilochius?	c. 263
Paul of Samosata	260/267–270/272
Domnus I/Dmonus	268–273
Timaeus	273–282
Cyril	283–303
Tyrannos/Tyrannion	304–314
Vitalis/Vitalius	314–320
St. Philogonus/Philogonius	320–323
Paulinus of Tyre	323–324
St. Eustathius	324–337
Paulinus?	c. 332
Eulalius	5 months? 331–333
Euphronius	333–334
Philaclus/Placentius	334–342
Stephanus I	342–344
Leontius	344–357

Eudoxius	358–359
Annias/Ammianus	c. 357
Euzoius/Eudozius/Eudoxius Patriarch of Constantinople	360 360–370
St. Meletius	361–381

Meletian Schism, 361–401; 381,

Dorotheus	rival, c. 370
Paulinus	Papal rival, c. 371
Vitalius?	rival, c. 376
Flavian I	381–404
Porphyrus/Porphyrius	404–412
Alexander	412–417
Theodotus	417–428
John I	428–442
Domnus II	442–449
Maximus II	449–455
Basil	456–458
Acacius	458–461
Martyrius	461–465
Peter the Fuller	465–466, 476–488
Julian	466–476
John II	488–490
Stephanus II	490–495
Stephen III?	c. 493
Callandion	495–496
John Codonatus?	c. 495

Palladius	496–498
Flavian II	498–512
Severus of Antioch deposed in schism, exiled in Egypt, recognized by Syrian Church	512–518, d. 538/546

Greek Orthodox/Melkite Patriarchs of Antioch

Paul I/II	518–521
Euphrosius/Euphrasius	521–526/528
Ephrem/Ephraim of Amid	526/528–546
Domnus III	546–561

4

The Roman Church Model

To BEGIN THE HISTORY of the building up of the church of Rome in worship and community is a joyous proceeding that soon becomes mired in the deceit, intrigue, political convention, and personal greed that marks the society and culture of the city of Rome itself. As Edward Gibbon states, "the theologian may indulge the pleasing task of describing Religion as she descended from Heaven, arrayed in her native purity. A more melancholy duty is imposed on the historian. He must discover the inevitable mixture of error and corruption, which she contracted in a long residence upon earth, among a weak and degenerate race of beings."[1] Rome has a long history dating from 750 BCE that reads more like a combined novel of Tom Clancy, and Stephen King. Even its mythical inception is marred by the description of being "the asylum for outlaws," and the city was shunned by the surrounding villages and inhabitants.[2]

THE ROMAN CHURCH FROM ITS INCEPTION
TO PAUL'S ARRIVAL

The church in Rome was probably started in 35 CE by the "visitors from Rome" (Acts 2:3) who returned from Pentecost with news of the resurrected Christ. Disciples such as Aquila and Priscilla became the Roman church's eyewitnesses to the finishing events of Christ's ministry in Jerusalem and the powerful testimony given to the disciples on Pentecost. The fact that apostolic presence was not part of Rome's beginning is evident. There is no evidence in Scriptural history or sectarian history that any of the apostles came to Rome prior to Paul's first imprisonment. We have good evidence in Hadrian's account that the Claudian expulsion of

1. Gibbon, *Decline and Fall*, 1:488.
2. Unger, *Unger's Bible Dictionary*, 934.

Jews from Rome in 49 CE was on the account of Jewish riots over one named "Chrestus."[3] We also conclude that Aquila and Priscilla's residency in Corinth was due to this expulsion of Jews. We also have a strange account from Tertullian and Clement in Eusebius concerning Tiberius's submittal of Jesus Christ before the senate to be recognized as God.[4]

It appears that by the time Paul finished his Epistle to the Romans Aquila and Priscilla had been reunited to the city of Rome, as Paul stated, "Greet Prisca and Aquila, my fellow workers in Christ Jesus" (Rom 16:3). This would place the completion of the Epistle at the time of Nero, who removed the Claudian ban of Jews in the city after his advancement to the purple through his mother Agrippina in 54 CE. Nero's family and household had somewhat of an affinity toward the Jews through Agrippina, his mother, and Poppaea, his γυνή, "wife."[5] Later, Nero murdered both his mother and wife in an effort to divert senatorial attention from himself to the Christians.

Cranfield establishes "the church of" Rome's beginnings as not due to apostolic "evangelistic enterprise" but by "Christians in the discharge of their ordinary secular duties or business."[6] As to Petrine foundation, Rome's claims seem obscure and false, as Cranfield states, "it is virtually certain that he [Peter] was not in Rome at the time that Paul was writing, and highly probable that ... he had never been there."[7] If any bishopric could claim to be the see of "Peter," it should be Antioch, as Eusebius and many of the ante-Nicene fathers establish Peter as the first bishop of Antioch and presiding over it up to his seizure and transport to Rome for his execution under Nero.[8] Any presumption on the part of Rome to claim to be the see of Peter should be viewed by historians as utter nonsense. Not once does Paul's letter mention Peter, nor any of the other twelve.

The list of the pillars of Rome's early church are found in the Epistle, chapter 16: Mary, Andronicus Junias, Ampliatus, Urbanus, Stachys, Apelles, Aristobolus, Herodian, Narcissus, Tryphaena, Tryphosa, Persis, Rufus, Asyncritus, Phlegon, Hermas, Patrobas, Hermes, Philologus, Julia,

---

3. Cranfield, *Romans*, 1:16.

4. Maier, *Eusebius*, 60–61.

5. Josephus *The Life* 3 (in *Works* 1:4, 8).

6. Cranfield, *Romans*, 1:17.

7. Ibid.

8. Maier, *Eusebius*, 94.

Nereus, Olympas. This list of early leaders and believers from Paul consist of those he knew in the church in Rome. Since he had not set foot in Rome prior to his writing, it would be safe and most prudent to assume that all those he names in his Epistle are alien to Rome.

Many of the above-mentioned names seem to be leadership imported from Syria or Asia Minor or Egypt. Such are Aristobolus, Herodian, and Rufus, who was the son of Simon the Cyrenian. "And they forced someone passing by into service—Simon, a Cyrenian, coming from *[the]* countryside (the father of Alexander and Rufus)—so that he should carry His cross" (Mark 15:21).

A strange account of the impact of the gospel on Rome is recorded in Eusebius, as written by Tertullian, who was a Roman jurist prior to his conversion:

> There was an old decree that no one should be consecrated as a god by an emperor before he had been approved by the senate.... Tiberius then, in whose time the name Christian came into the world, when this doctrine was reported to him from Palestine, where it began, communicated it to the senate, plainly indicating that he favored the doctrine. The senate, however, rejected it, because it had not itself reviewed it; but Tiberius stuck to his own opinion and threatened death to any who accused the Christians.[9]

Paul Maier states that "there is no record in secular sources of Tiberius's support of Christianity."[10] However, in Tacitus's *Annals*, the description of the evil and corruption of Tiberius seems to be toward his moderate behaviors specifically in these regards:

1. He discouraged the deification of past and present emperors.

2. He persecuted those who may have opposed the doctrine.

3. His personal humility in which he approached his title as Augustus was, as Tacitus stated, dishonoring to the office.

4. He became reclusive and retired in retreat during his latter reign.

Many have criticized the accuracy of this account in Tacitus's history concerning Tiberius. However, the most abhorrent actions of Tiberius according to Tacitus were based on Tacitus's disdain of Christianity. He

9. Tertullian *Defense* 5, in Maier, *Eusebius*, 61.
10. Ibid.

describes Tiberius as a humble man not wishing to be adored or deified, which Tacitus explains as reckless and dishonoring to his divine office. He also criticizes Tiberius for eliminating certain nobles and kin (Germanicus). Tacitus also criticizes Tiberius for becoming a recluse in the later portion of his reign. I might draw one to the Elucidation of this passage. The jurist Tertullian would have had access to legal documents of the realm, and his apologetic was addressed to the Emperor Macrinus, therefore he would have been sure of his sources, as "It is not supposable that such a man would have hazarded his bold appeal to the records, in remonstrating with the Senate and in the very faces of the Emperor and his colleagues, had he not known that the evidence was irrefragable" (indisputable).[11]

In another account of Tiberius's life written by the biographer Seutonius, he describes the first marriage of Tiberius as being an extremely happy union. The law of the Romans assumed that if a wife became pregnant within the first year of childbirth it was assumed that she had an adulterous relationship, and the husband was obliged by law to put her away by divorce. She could then remarry, and she was not to have any contact with her former husband. When this happened to Vispania Agrippina after the birth of Drussus, Tiberius was reluctant to divorce her. However, the courts stepped in and made it happen. Later, after a few years had gone by, Tiberius made contact with Vispania. Weeping in regret of the divorce, he sadly spoke to Vispania. But the courts stepped in and put a restraining order on him, preventing him from ever making contact with his love and first wife. As Seutonius writes, "he loved Vispania and strongly disapproved of Julia" (his second wife).[12] Such descriptions of Tiberius constituted the many railings against him. The society of Rome deemed his behavior uncontainable. But would his behavior have been objectionable to the Christian society then, and today?

Based on the problems encountered between the followers of "Chrestus" and the Jews during the reign of Claudius, the Jews were banished from Rome. It would be very likely that Claudius had made his decision to banish all Jews from Rome based on Tiberius's appeal to the Senate and his declaration to protect the Christians from persecution. During this banishment Aquila and Priscilla settled in Corinth, met Paul

11. Holmes, "Elucidation" 4 of Tertullian's *Against Praxeas* 5.
12. Seutonius *The Twelve Caesars* (Graves trans., 112).

on the mission field, and took a leading role in the church there. This banishment lasted from 49 CE to 54 CE, when Nero lifted the ban, allowing the Jews to return. In the context of Paul's Epistle to the Romans, we find that Paul reeducates the Roman Gentiles by writing, "But if their transgression is the riches of the world, and their failure the riches of the Gentiles, how much more their fullness! For I speak to you, the Gentiles, to the degree that I am indeed an apostle of Gentiles, I glorify my ministry" (Rom 11:12–13).

Early Christianity cannot be understood apart from its social setting, neither in Jerusalem nor in Rome. Christianity in the church was not changing social conventions until the impact of conversion had its full result. Set societies would not make drastic changes based on experience alone, but upon educational institution. Rome would not change overnight by conversion but would as the teaching of the apostles permeated the church. In fact, Rome would hardly be changed, as Leland writes, "The extraordinary tenacity and earnestness with which the Tuscans have clung to these fragments of their old faith is quite in accordance with their ancient character."[13] It has been suggested that the old order was a difficult setting to crack in Rome, where there was no love lost for things Greek, philosophies and the like, but concerning the pagan Etruscan culture Leland postulates, "to a person of humanity and tender feelings there is something very touching or indescribably pitiful in the manner which the people in Europe clung to their old gods and resisted Christianity."[14]

The early Roman church was already exercising a preemptory view of its elevated status because Rome was the heart of the empire. The Scriptures of the Old Testament had already condemned homosexual practice and yet Rome had for years encouraged effeminate behavior as a religious practice in the Temple of Vesta and in other Roman religious institutions. It was the law and authority of the caesar as pontifex maximus to assure that the male priests of Vesta were effeminate, or castrated. The household of caesar already practiced a eunuch-driven civil administration.

The Greek and Roman gods provided the backdrop for the cultural behavior of the Roman citizen. There is an account of a Greek aristocrat instructing his young son how to act at the *skolia* (symposium, party, a place, event where songs are performed). The aristocratic father is asked

13. Leland, *Etruscan Magic*, 11.
14. Ibid., 98.

the question of how to act as an aristocrat, to which he replies, "elegantly." He later was railed against by his neighbors when in the course of the evening he committed acts of debauched brutality in conjunction with his party evening.[15] The corruption in the civil administration, daily routine, and palace of Rome, was well established. "Magicians and necromancers abounded, and were liberally patronized. The ancient simplicity and contentment were exchanged for boundless avarice and prodigality. Morality and chastity, so beautifully symbolized in the household ministry of the virgin Vesta, yielded to vice and debauchery"[16] Concerning the state of Rome, Seneca writes, "Rome is full of crime and vices. More are committed than can be cured by force. There is an immense struggle for iniquity. Crimes are no longer hidden, but open before the eyes. Innocence is not only rare, but nowhere."[17]

Another issue seen from Paul's writing is the conduct of the church in Rome. It could be true that the first Christian groups in Rome were swayed by the presence of Simon Magus; according to Eusebius, Clement, Justin, and Irenaeus, when he came to Rome he was celebrated as a god. "Whatever is more disgusting than the foulest crime imaginable is surpassed by the utterly repulsive heresy of these men, who, drenched in vice, make sport of wretched women."[18] Among the practicing ascetic Gnostics was the even more prevalent practice of communal property. Groups of Gnostics would have all properties in common, even the communal use of women and slaves. Hence, Paul writes,

> For this reason, you are without excuse [or, defense], O person, every [one] judging, for in what you judge [or, pass sentence on] the other, you condemn yourself, for the same [things] you, the one judging, are practicing! But we know that the judgment of God is according to truth upon the ones practicing such [things]. But do you think this, O person (the one judging the ones practicing such things yet doing them), that you will escape the judgment of God? Or do you despise [or, think lightly of] the riches of His goodness and tolerance and patience, failing to understand [or, disregarding] that the kindness of God leads you to repentance? But according to your hardness [fig., obstinacy] and impenitent heart, you are

15. Boardman, Griffen, and Murray *Oxford History of the Classical World*, 218–19.

16. Schaff, *History of the Christian Church*, 1:83.

17. Seneca *De Ira* 2.8 (Schaff trans., 84).

18. Maier, *Eusebius*, 72.

storing up for yourself wrath in *[the]* day of wrath and of revelation and of *[the]* righteous judgment of God. (Rom 2:1–5)

This lack of confidence in Roman leadership on the part of the apostles is evident because the leadership in the Roman church were imported from Syria (Antioch), Asia Minor (Phrygia, Ephesus), Macedonia (Philippi, Berea), and Achaia (Athens). According to the record of the List of the Popes, the first four bishops of Rome (Linus, Anacletus, Clement, Eugarius) were appointed by Peter and Paul, and were not native Romans.[19] It appears that the apostolic authorities' lack of confidence in Roman church leadership stemmed from this early perversion of the gospel through these Gnostic influences. The Gnostics in all regions had great appeal to two different sympathies in lifestyle. The ascetic group appealed to the Jews and the licentious group appealed to the Gentiles involved in the mystery religions. But in Rome the citizens faced an even greater danger from the very ground itself. We have a similar effect presented in the Old Testament when the Lord speaks to Cain after he had killed his brother Abel. "The voice of your brother's blood is crying to me from the ground"(Gen. 5:10). The ending of this effect is a curse: "now you are cursed from the ground" (Gen 5:11). As Sodom and Gomorrah and Canaan were cursed from the ground, so it was in Rome. This effect of the debauchery of past generations on the citizens of the city was evident in its day.

ROME FROM PAUL'S IMPRISONMENT TO PETER'S AND PAUL'S DEATHS

The courage of the church in Rome according to the Scriptures is suspect. In his letter Paul had mentioned to Timothy that all of those in Rome were ashamed of his chains, and he asked that they not be held to account for it (2 Tim 4:16). That happened during his first defense in which he won the day, yet many departed from him, trying to save their reputations. During Paul's imprisonment the church of Rome's reaction to Paul's presence was mixed, as he writes to the Philippians, "Some to be sure are preaching Christ even from envy and strife, but some also from good will; the latter do it out of love, knowing that I am appointed for the defense of the gospel; the former proclaim Christ out of selfish ambition, rather than

---

19. Kelly, *Oxford Dictionary of the Popes*, 6–8.

from pure motives, thinking to cause me distress in my imprisonment" (Phil 1:15–17 nasb).

Hermas,[20] who is said to have been the brother of Pius, bishop of Rome in 140 ce, speaks in his writing, the *Shepherd of Hermas* of himself as a Roman freedman, initially the slave of a noble lady, Rhoda. His concern lies in the sins that have occurred post-baptism, and he relates a dream or vision of a tower being built with stones some from the sea and some from the earth. The stones from the sea are the saints of the church, having been martyred for the Lord's name, and usable for the tower (the church). The stones from the earth are not usable yet, as they are put aside, but not put away. These are the "lapsed" who are truly repentant yet not able to be absolved.[21] This development in the Roman church shows some of the issues facing Rome and its move toward sanctification by good works.

"Greet Andronicus and Junia, my relatives *[or, close companions]* and my fellow-prisoners, who are well-known by *[or, among]* the apostles, who also have been in Christ before me" (Rom 16:7). It appears that Paul has several relatives in the church of Rome. He names Andronicus and Junia as *syngeneis* (connected by birth), as he also does Herodian. Of Adronicus and Junia, he records them as being "his fellow prisoners." This would suppose that Paul, at the time of writing the sixteenth chapter, was already in the custody of the Romans in Jerusalem or in Caesarea, and Andronicus and Junia were in custody in Rome. This is not without corroboration from other sources, as Flavius Josephus sometime in the late 50s or early 60s was sent to Rome to petition Nero for the release from

---

20. Confusion surrounds the writing of the *Shepherd of Hermas*. F. F. Bruce in his book *The New Testament Documents* ascribes the writing itself to around 115 (p. 17), while his Canon of Scripture attributes the writing to Hermas the brother of Pius the Bishop of Rome sometime around 140 (p. 166). But his earlier date is likely since the issues at hand would be attributable results of Domitian's pogrom against the church in the late first century. Does that rule out the writing as penned by Hermas the brother of Pius? Not at all, as Hermas himself was considered an older man and noted as the writer of the "Shepherd" in 140. In the Allegory the description of Hermas as the freedman of Rhoda depicts a young man with a young man's fancy toward Rhoda. It is unlikely that the Hermas who is addressed in Romans 16 is the writer since the timing would make the author about sixty years old by the second century and seventy-five to one hundred when the Allegory was more than likely written. It was not included in the canon because of its later date. Tertullian and Irenaeus in the late second century quoted from the work, and both categorized the writing as noncanonical.

21. González, *A History of Christian Thought*, 1:87.

custody in Rome of some Jews who were seized and sent to the capital.[22] Josephus also mentioned that he departed from Caesarea in two ships which encountered a storm, and of which one is shipwrecked.[23] Could this be the same storm that shipwrecked Paul on Malta or the same journey that took Paul to Rome?

Paul also refers to Herodian in like manner, referring to him as connected by birth, making Paul part of the Herodian line, and yet through one of his parents he is a Benjamite.

PAUL'S CONTACT WITH SENECA

It is likely that the philosopher Seneca had some contact with Paul in possibly four locations:

1. During Paul's court appearance before Gallio in Achaia: Seneca was on Gallio's council, having been redeemed from his exile to Corsica. Seneca was the brother of Gallio.

2. During Paul's first defense in Rome: Paul was likely to have rented a room from the praetorian prefect under the law of *praefectus urbi*,[24] which authorized the praetorian prefect to house the citizens of the Roman Empire coming before the emperor to state their case. The prefect at that time was Vitrasius Polio, Seneca's uncle. Earlier he had been prefect of Egypt.

3. During Paul's defense before Nero: Seneca was one of Nero's advisors, along with Burrhus, who would preview all of the cases brought before the emperor. Burrhus and Seneca in 65 CE were instructed to commit suicide on the orders of Nero, who held them accountable for the Piso rebellion.

4. Finally, tradition has it that Seneca wrote six letters to Paul. The manuscripts date from the ninth century, but Tertullian alludes to letters of Seneca and stated that Seneca was "our own," while Jerome quotes from the letters that were extant in his day.[25]

---

22. Josephus *The Life* 3.
23. Ibid.
24. Sherwin-White, *Roman Law*, 109.
25. Correspondence of Paul and Seneca.

This brings about an understanding that during the Neronian empire many politicians, philosophers, and nobles were closet Christians, composing moral treatises and philosophies that followed the faith without mentioning Christ or those who were being dragged to their deaths in Nero's rage against the sect. The Neronian persecution may have prompted the attempt on his life through the Piso conspiracy, for those of the faith in Nero's court, in the senate, and of the elite of the empire were not exempt from the wrath of the demented emperor.

Erroneously, it appears that soon after the destruction of the temple of Jerusalem in 70 CE, Rome and the Christians residing there presumed a secessionist view of the mantle of Israel and God's departure from the Jewish focus, thus promoting a rudimentary "replacement theology." It does appear that the churches in all of the evangelized Mediterranean where led to believe that the capital of the Roman Empire held a preeminent role in the leadership of the church and the receiving of the grace of God. With such notions came all of the theological baggage that the Jewish churches espoused. As centuries progressed the church of Rome appeared in practice to be James's church in Jerusalem, in the monarchial polity, and in the theology Ebion (Ebionism, Jacobitism).

THE INFLUENCE AND IMPACT OF CONSTANTINE ON THE WESTERN ROMAN CHURCH

Constantine had a profound effect on all of Christianity, but his impact in the West was minimized by the development of the "New Rome," Constantinople, and the arrogance of the bishopric of Rome. Constantine's conversion opened up the legitimacy of Christianity. In 312 CE the Milan policy was proclaimed by imperial edict. Constantine's edict declared the empire to be tolerant of all cults and that all properties taken from the Christians in the last persecutions were to be restored. Christianity became a popular front in Rome toward the promotion of unprincipled men. The Milan policy and the edict of 315 had a profound effect on the empire because the Christian clergy were exempt from all taxes, from military and public service, and the bishops became the chief magistrates to hear land cases after the Milan policy.

The elevation of the bishops in political and jurist authority in the realm brought all sorts of corrupt political forms including simony and nepotism. F. F. Bruce states, "where church leaders were able to exercise political as well as spiritual authority, they did not enjoy an immunity from the universally corrupting tendency of power—a tendency which presents an even more displeasing spectacle in Christians than it does in other people, because it clashes so with the first principles of Christianity."[26]

Constantine, however, countered this effect in Rome by moving his capital to Byzantium (Constantinople) in 326. His reasoning surely was that Rome ultimately was not defensible, and the migration of Germanic hordes into the peninsula was a great threat to the security of the empire. This was an easy decision, as the bulk of all the wealth in the empire was in the east and in the south. But to make it even clearer that Rome was not Constantine's favorite city, the Western capital was moved to Milan, where the palace and the princes who were ruling the West could be defended with certainty.

The palace of Fausta was given as a residence to Sylvester, the bishop of Rome. This piece of history was used as propaganda later in the eighth century to signify that the intention of Constantine to give the "sovereignty of all Italy and the west" to the pope was established.[27] Twofold was this lie, first that the mantel of government in the West was passed to the spiritual authority, and second, that the spiritual authority was the see of Peter in Rome.

THE INFLUENCE AND IMPACT OF CONSTANTIUS ON THE WESTERN ROMAN CHURCH

Constantius was a thorough Arian, who imposed on the church a reinstatement of Arius and exiled any bishop who did not recognize the reinstatement. This included Athanasius, bishop of Alexandria. Constantius saw that the unity sought by Constantine was good for the church and for the empire, but chose the path of Arianism over Nicaeanism. After the death of Constans, who held a Nicaean faith, Constantius started a pogrom of removing any bishop who opposed the reinstatement of Arius, even posthumously, but more relevant his reinstated doctrines. In Rome this set the stage for the later Arian Gothic kingdoms to be well established, having a foundation in Arian thought and doctrine that was already prevalent in the West.

26. Bruce, *Advance of Christianity*, 293.
27. Ibid., 299.

When Julian was just appointed caesar in the West, he observed his cousin, Contantius, removing Liberius from Rome for supporting Athanasius and Nicea and deposing Hilary for the same reason. This certainly impressed on Julian the idea of controlling the church by controlling the appointees to the bishoprics. Being well versed in the ancient religion of Rome, Julian saw the title of Pontifex Maximus as a way to combat the church that he despised. Julian soon reinstated Liberius as a co-bishop with the purpose of dividing the church of Rome into two bitterly disputed factions, and thus weakened its unity and resolve without arousing Constantius's notice.

THE INFLUENCE AND IMPACT OF JULIAN THE APOSTATE ON THE WESTERN ROMAN CHURCH

In understanding the influence Julian had on the empire and the church, which was one entity at the time, the words of G. W. Bowersock are appropriate: "One must reject, firmly and dispassionately, the lonely hero struggling against the onslaught of corrupt Christianity . . . and the courageous friend of the Jews. Julian was none of these."[28] The disagreeable impact of Julian, who was called the Apostate by the Eastern Church, has been greater felt in the West as he was on the throne for eight more years in Milan than in the East. Observing the authority of Constantius in 355, who deposed Bishop Liberius for defending Athanasius and the Nicaean faith, banished him to Boreora, Thrace. In 356 Julian deposed Hilary, the bishop of Poitiers, to Phrygia, who was one of the chief defenders of the Nicaean faith in the West.[29]

Many historians credit that act to Constantius but fail to include a clear picture of Constantius's role in the administration of the West. Constantius had found himself embroiled in wars on two fronts. In the East he battled with the Persian kings for those last eight years of his reign, and in the West, he left the full administration of the Western empire in the hands of Julian, who was also engaged in war against the Frankish pagan kings. Avoiding the scrutiny from the Arian East, Julian claimed to be a Christian caesar, or at least did not declare otherwise. Constantius did not object to Julian's moves, because Constantius had established an

---

28. Bowersock, *Julian the Apostate*, 2.
29. Bruce, *Advance of Christianity*, 318.

Arian state in the East, deposing Athanasius in Alexandria by replacing him with George, an Arian.

After Constantius deposed Liberius and replaced the patris at Rome with a Sophist named Felix (the best that can be said of Felix would be that he was Arian). Felix won over the former secretary of Liberius, Damasus, and brought into the Roman see a plethora of anti-Christian religious symbols and practices. Later Julian reinstated Liberius and Athanasius to bring back into the "Galilean religion" opposing parties that would combat the unity that his uncle Constantine had established at Nicaea and also to interject old Roman religion into the fabric of the church. He felt that if Christianity was divided it would destroy itself and leave a void for the traditional gods of Rome to fill.

During this time period Julian won the allegiance of the legions by promoting, and filling his armies with pagan authority. Using his military, he starved entire cities of pagan Franks until they became his adherents and gave wealth, fame and authority to their leaders as a bonus of his magnanimity. By the end of his eight-year reign as caesar in the West, Julian had more than seven legions of pagan troops participating in bloody sacrifices to the goddess Cybil and the god Mithra. To those soldiers who appreciated his generosity to the troops, he was a god in stature, but to those soldiers who would maintain their faith and Christian testimony a *loquax tolpa*, "a talking mole."[30] Gibbon quotes one of the Julian orations, in which he consecrates the "honour of Cybil, the mother of the gods, who required from her effeminate priests the bloody sacrifice." Gibbon goes on to state that when Julian was a boy, he "so rashly performed the madness" of this ritual that to the pagan world he was most pious.[31] To his sophist friends Libanius and Ammianus, Julian was the height and epitome of human virtue. After all, he was the strongest hope for the tradition of Rome to be reborn and their pagan ambitions to be restored and realized. "Pagans in every province" had hope in his future greatness while he was still a youth, and "from the zeal and virtues of their royal proselyte they fondly expected the cure of every evil and the restoration of every blessing," when Julian "confessed that he was ambitious to attain a situation in which he might be useful to his country and his religion."[32] Yet even his

30. Bowersock, *Julian the Apostate*, 13.

31. Gibbon, *Decline and Fall*, 2:411.

32. Ibid., 2:418.

most deplorable of character traits were not hidden from his friends and fans. Ammianus even remarked of the cruelty in which he pursued those who "were in his way."[33] True to his sophistry, "he grew accustomed to saying and to practicing what he did not believe. For ten years he comported himself publicly as a Christian while worshipping the pagan gods."[34] It was only on the death of Constantius that he revealed himself to the empire as a pagan emperor.

Gregory Nazianzen said of Julian that "the church had far more to fear from enemies within than enemies without."[35] Athanasius also stated that Julian was "just a dark cloud that was passing over." But that, I'm afraid, was just an encouragement to the faithful Christians in the East, because the damage had already been accomplished in the West.

Julian's religion was ritual and sacrifice. He and his counselors emphasized the rigor of ceremonial practice and understood that the philosophic goal of the true religion of the Hellenes was only accomplished by rituals performed in mass.[36] He implied that the population could not fully understand the true religion and true philosophy of Hellenism and was obliged by the gods to perform it. All over the empire Julian reestablished the temples of pagan deities for the purpose of instituting their blood sacrifices. In the edict of 363 he returned all properties held by the Christian churches that once were temples to ancient deities. He felt that the Galileans were not sufficiently intelligent to understand the Hellenistic philosophy and could be swayed by sophistry to perform the rites, making the blood sacrifice into a bloodless sacrifice. I am sure this was his intention by deposing the bishops of Alexandria, Antioch, Jerusalem, and earlier Rome, substituting sophists in the posts. He continued his pogrom against the Christians by banning them from teaching philosophy, rhetoric, and classical literature, saying, "how can the Galileans teach that which they do not believe."[37]

Julian turned a blind eye to the murder of George of Alexandria at the hands of a mob of Hellenistic pagans inspired by the aggressiveness of the new emperor. He stated that George deserved what he had received, but

33. Schaff, *History of the Christian Church*, 3:58–59.

34. Bowersock, *Julian the Apostate*, 18.

35. Schaff, *History of the Christian Church*, 3:59.

36. Bowersock, *Julian the Apostate*, 86.

37. Ibid., 84.

encouraged the Alexandrian pagans to extirpate the Christians legally. He made it illegal in the empire to conduct a funeral in daylight, stating that the dead belonged to the darkness of the underworld and it is sacrilegious and a defilement that a body would be exposed to the light. The pagan societies became so enamored with such progress that soon inscriptions on milestones proclaiming "one God" proclaimed "one Julian."[38]

"The vast Roman state could not easily and quickly lay aside its heathen traditions and customs; it perpetuated them under Christian names."[39] That which was left in Rome after Julian could be summed up by using this sophistic method: Cybele could be substituted for Mary, who is deemed the "mother of God" in Rome; and Mithra, the sun god, being one of Cybele's offspring, could be substituted for Jesus. Future chapters will include some of the pagan symbolism adopted by Rome, such as "the sun of righteousness," the use of the eye of Horus, and the use of the upside down cross.

But what is sophistry and how did it mask paganism and infiltrate the Christian orthodoxy of the West? Over the millennia the meaning of the word *sophist* has changed considerably. Its earliest meaning seems to refer to someone who gave *sophia* to his students, that is, wisdom made from knowledge. However, it is not likely that the term was used to describe an honorable individual dedicated to the education and the bringing of "wisdom" (*sophia*) to young minds. In the Greek classical period, the second half of the fifth century BCE, and especially at Athens, "sophist" came to be applied to a group of thinkers and speakers who employed rhetoric to achieve their purposes at any cost, specifically to persuade or convince others of their prowess in the art. The rhetorical skills utilized in jurisprudence became of great value due to the continued litigations of the day in Athens and other Hellenized cities and principalities.

> Due to the importance of such skills in the litigious social life of Athens, practitioners of such skills often commanded very high fees. The practice of taking fees, coupled with the willingness of many sophists to use their rhetorical skills to pursue unjust lawsuits, eventually led to a decline in respect for practitioners of this form of teaching and the ideas and writings associated with it.[40]

38. Ibid., 91.

39. Gibbon, *Decline and Fall*, 3:358.

40. Boyles, *Sophistry*, no page.

This practice continued to the Constantinian era and increased the Sophist's fee base in Constantine's empire because of the Milan policy and other laws that gave Christian leaders advantage in due process. A skilled rhetorician could win the day in court for a client against the backdrop of a legal system tipping toward the Christians. But these rhetorical skills, which were associated with classical pagan gods, and the mindset to win the debate at any cost were particularly appealing to the old Roman order that desperately sought to be in power again.

Julian's issue with the Christian church stems from his immersion in sophistry. He viewed the legitimacy of any religion by its age and its ability to hold the public order (*nomos*) for centuries. The classical sophist Critias asserted that the gods were contrived by "governments to insure that men would believe that everything done on earth whether openly or secretly was seen by the gods and would consequently be discouraged from violating the laws of state."[41] Julian surmised that since Christianity was a "new" religion, it has no legitimate reason for existing in the Roman Empire, and realizing that he held the honor of pontifex maximus, he regarded himself as the authority to put an end to illegitimate religions. The religions of value to the realm were the old ones—Mithraism, Cybelism, the Greek and Roman pantheon, and even Judaism, which was recognized by the Roman Republic—all of these were the backbone of the strength and rise of the empire itself. He deemed Judaism less worthy. Nevertheless, prior to his campaign in Persia that removed him from the earth he had begun the work of restoring the temple in Jerusalem, not because he preferred the religion, but because he felt it was more legitimate than Christianity, and Judaism generally opposed the Christian truths.[42] Yet the testimony of even his pagan friends suggested that God would not allow the reconstruction of the temple in Jerusalem, as the construction crews and the site were subject to all forms of catastrophic events before hope was given up.[43] Julian supposed that the enemies of his enemies must be his friends or at least his allies.

Julian's influence in the church tells us of the long-lasting effect of the edicts of the emperor as seen in the usage of Christian terminology in a neo-pagan milieu. "The epigraphic texts reflect the religious struggle

41. Dunkle, "Classical Origins of Western Culture."
42. Gibbon, *Decline and Fall*, 2:436–37.
43. Schaff, *History of the Christian Church*, 3:54–57.

of [Julian] and the subtle ways in which the language of Christianity was converted to the service of revived paganism."[44] His legacy is most demonstrated in the succession of the bishops of Rome after the deposition of Liberius and the appointment of Felix, the usurpation of Damasus, the false orthodoxy of Jerome, the exercise and use of sophistic methodology to disguise the Roman pagan theology, the legal system as Christian, and the elevation of the ancient pagan gods as distinctly Christian.

Julian's appointees to the bishopric of Rome provided a long and lasting channel for developed error and heresy. Damasus, the secretary of the anti-pope Felix, insisted on the *Theotokos* doctrine being added to the church. He was also the first to employ the use of thugs to gain the papal crown by killing 160 followers of his opponent.[45]

THE DILEMMA OF CHRISTIANITY COEXISTING WITH THE EMPIRICAL THEOLOGY OF ROME

Julian had reestablished Roman imperial theology to the church of Rome without it noticing. In Rome that was not difficult because most of the Roman and Italian aristocratic families were still inclined to embrace the old republic and the old religion. As Phillip Schaff writes,

> Especially in Rome, many of the oldest and most respectable families for a long time still adhered to the heathen traditions, and the city appears to have preserved until the latter part of the fourth century a hundred and fifty-two temples and a hundred and eighty-three smaller chapels and altars of patron deities. But advocates of the old religion (Theimestius, Libanius, Symmachus) limited themselves to the claim of toleration.[46]

Julian's greatest success was in the West, but in the East, after he established his palace in Antioch, he was despised and ridiculed by the Christian population. The Roman imperial theology that Julian tried to reinstate could not coexist with Christianity in the orthodox East, because the office of the Augustus held the high seat of theology. He was the "king of the gods."[47] Libations of wine and bread were given to the image of the emperor, while behind his image was the image of the gods,

---

44. Bowersock, *Julian the Apostate*, 11.

45. Kelly, *Popes*, 33.

46. Schaff, *History of the Christian Church*, 3:61.

47. Showalter, *Panegyric of Pliny*, 5–6.

whom the people gave verbal supplications.[48] The emperor then would receive direction or counsel from the gods through the oracles (words given to prophets and prophetesses), which could only be interpreted by the Augustus and were categorically applied, ignored, or adjusted according to his interpretation. This legal authority granted to the Augustus gave him infallibility in all his edicts, decisions, and actions. The gods were fallible, but the Augustus was infallible. Such infallibility, however, was only enforceable by the support of the military. To accomplish his agenda the Augustus bundled the powers ascribed to him at different times.[49] This gave the emperor tools to withstand any challenge to his authority. Hence, he could keep the senate or any other pre-empirical corporation at bay while he mustered support from the military. The Augustus was known as *pater patreia*, "father of the fatherland."

All positions held in the Roman Empire were civil service positions and religious titles or posts at the same time. The pontifex maximus (the emperor) held the position of high priest of priests, which enabled him to appoint from the civil service each priest to each god. Those positions were steps in the careers of prominent nobles, imperial family, and those who would support the emperor and establish the Pax Romana in every province. This Roman imperial theology was then a true church-state. But the point of conflict with Orthodox Christianity is that the risen Christ was the Head of the Church, whereas the Roman model made a "vicar" the head of the church, because it should be a visible head.

POINTS OF COLLISION BETWEEN THE OLD ROMAN IMPERIAL THEOLOGY AND THE TRUE ORTHODOX CHURCH

Old Rome found itself in confrontation with the new Christian order, and the true orthodoxy was unable to tolerate the empirical theology in the following points:

1. The Augustus was infallible: "The bundle of powers at different times"[50] included the edict, bull; the titles of *Pater Patreia* (father of the fatherland), *Dominus* (Lord), imperator to military; the *dies imperii* (day of accession); the *praenomen* (surpassed or first name)

48. Ibid., 5.
49. Levick, *Claudius*, 41.
50. Ibid.

84

and *cognomen* Caesar (family name); and the recognition of *privates cum imperio* (emperor waking or sleeping), and the authority of Consul.

2. The Pontifex Maximus appointed priests (bishops and clergy).

3. Tribute was paid to the Augustus as the king of the gods.

4. There was no direct supplication to the gods because all are to make *supplicatio* through the Augustus.

5. The god was subordinate to the Augustus.

6. Sophistic methodology was used toward the goal of Pax Romana.

7. The senatorial struggle with the emperor was tied up in religion. Pliny gave Trajan advice not to reject the consular position presented by the senate so as not to downplay the importance of the senate.

8. Tiberius saw the balance of peace with the princep (caesar) and senate and empire as being a "stick on the water" (the water being knights, plebs, provincials) and thought that such a balance was like having a "wolf by the ears."[51] The provincial dignitaries were given holdings and status in Rome (Simon Magus was a Roman provincial); Pax Romana included maintaining the peace by appeasing the provincial deities, which were renamed for Roman worship so that the people were at peace with Rome because they could also worship them in Rome. The Orthodox church found contention with the provincials who were appeasing local gods by stamping out the new faith where they could.

9. The emperors in the new religion walked a crooked path with Roman canon law.

10. Roman imperial theology made Roman law foundational and Christianity secondary.

Romanum imperium pertit, "the Roman Empire disappeared," was only true in certain parts of Italy.[52] Our history of the Roman Empire is usually reflected by those parts and not by the greater Roman Empire that endured in the East until 1453. But in the West, the church of Rome took the authority of the Augustus after Leo declared himself to be Pontifex

51. Ibid., 8.
52. Webster and Brown, *Transformation of the Roman World*, 9.

Maximus. There is a difference between a church-state and a state-church, as the West assumed the prior and the East held to the later.

In Augustine's warning to the church, he iterates that the church should beware of adding to the Creed—the Nicene Creed of 325—or subtracting from it:

> It is underneath these few words, therefore, which are thus set in order in the Creed, that most heretics have endeavored to conceal their poisons; whom divine mercy has withstood, and still withstands, by the instrumentality of spiritual men, who have been worthy not only to accept and apprehend it by the enlightenment imparted by the Lord. But the handling of the faith is of service for the protection of the Creed ... but that it may guard the matters which are retained in the Creed against the insidious assaults ... of the heretics, by means of catholic authority and a more entrenched defense.[53]

This treatment by Augustine followed the writing of his work on the Trinity, which stood out as a defense of the Nicene faith. His warning to the church militant is then to beware of any who would revise the Creed of 325. Augustine made it clear that the Creed was established to be left alone and intact. The later additions of the *filioque* clause, the description of the Holy Spirit, and the deletion of the anathemas, in light of Augustine's writing, reveal a clear purpose to dash to pieces the monarchy of Christ and establish the Arian understanding of the Trinity.

THE STRUGGLE OF AUGUSTINE WITH THE BISHOP OF ROME

In his epic work *City of God*, Augustine chastens the church of Rome for returning or trying to return to the gods of Rome for repose from the woes of its many sieges. He states emphatically that if the gods were able to deliver the population from the woes of war, why did the Greeks fall to the Persians or the Egyptians to the Babylonians? He entreated the churchmen of Rome to be thankful that Alaric and other conquerors had a regard for the church because they did not destroy it, but they purposed to preserve the buildings and the clergy of the Roman see. But within the allegorical writings of Augustine other questions were posed, other concerns voiced: could the Arian kings reconstruct the Julian ideal of the priesthood? Could the Arian kings establish the Roman pantheon

---

53. Augustine, *Treatise on Faith and the Creed* 1.1.4–5 (Salmond trans., 321).

in Rome? Could the sophistry of the Alexandrian system replace the true God with other gods—the infallibility of the Pontifex Maximus, the curia, the veneration of Mary as the mother of God? Was Hermes role leading the dead ones to the underworld likewise Mary's role? What changes would be made in the church that would destroy the Nicene faith in the West?

Augustine saw the preterism or partial preterism of the situation in which Rome found itself. Augustine reasoned that just as there were ten plagues in Egypt that allowed the Jews to start to depart toward the land of Canaan, there were ten kings who brought persecution on the early church. The eleventh plague was the pursuit of the Jews by pharaoh's army and its annihilation in the Red Sea. So explained Augustine that the eleventh plague to bring the church to the promised land will come from the antichrist. He went on to explain that the antichrist is the Arian persecution of the West, by the Visigothic and the Ostrogothic kings.[54] He also could be referring to the persecution that Valens initiated on the Eastern churches and the Homoousian party as he reminded readers that John said there were "many antichrists." Augustine viewed the antichrist that John revealed as an institution of Arian doctrine. He stated clearly that the Arian doctrine of adoptionism and subjectionism was the same as saying, "The Christ did not come in the flesh." This one who says there was a time when the Son did not exist, "he is the antichrist" (1 John 4:3). Was Augustine condemning the see of Rome as the synagogue of the antichrist?

DAMASUS AND JEROME: PAPAL ELEVATION OF VIOLENCE

Two of Augustine's contemporaries in Rome are Damasus and Jerome. Damasus gained the bishopric of Rome by hiring thugs to massacre the followers of his opponent Ursinus in the church. Over 180 of his supporters were destroyed at the hands of his brigands. The history written to preserve the sainthood of Damasus and Jerome says that Ursinus propagated an intense civil war and that Damasus was not involved in the massacre, but the civil authorities acted on their own and therefore were justified in their actions and confirmation of the infallible pope.

But the administration of Damasus became far worse with time. The foundation of Damasus's administration was based in the following:

---

54. Augustine, *City of God* 18.52.

1. the promotion of veneration of the saints;

2. the promotion of the veneration of relics;

3. the veneration of Mary as the *Theotokos*;

4. the promotion of a Latin only (Vulgata) text to replace the Greek and Hebrew Scriptures;

5. the destruction of opposition to Roman preeminence;

6. the establishment of the Roman see as a wealthy and opulent power.

"Critics noted his opulent manner," and "Damasus allegedly cultivated the attentions of rich Roman ladies in particular,[55] and acquired a reputation for" not only their sexual favors, but also their "wealth."[56] An edict was written by Valentinian condemning such practices by all the clergy of Rome, as Gibbon writes,

> The strict regulations which have been framed by the wisdom of modern legislators to restrain the wealth and avarice of the clergy, may be originally deduced from the example of the emperor Valentinian. His edict, addressed to Damasus, bishop of Rome, was publicly read in the churches of the city. He admonished the ecclesiastics and monks not to frequent the houses of widows and virgins; and menaced their disobedience with the animadversion of the civil judge. The directors (patriarch, bishops, and abbots) were no longer permitted to receive any gift, or legacy, or inheritance, from the liberality of his spiritual-daughter: every testament contrary to this edict was declared null and void; and the illegal donation was confiscated for the use of the treasury.[57]

This was not the first intervention the emperor needed, for it was just a couple of years prior that Valentinian sent in troops to the city to quell the mayhem caused by the party of Damasus at his "election" by force. "No wonder, they thought, he had been prepared to stop at nothing, even mass murder, in order to win such treasures as his personal prize."[58]

According to the Vatican's story, Damasus's administration established Roman ecclesiastical domination and greatness for the Roman see,

---

55. These ladies were of the aristocratic families that promoted the old Roman religion to restore the empire to its former greatness with the help of the gods.

56. Davidson, *A Public Faith*, 121.

57. Gibbon, Gibbon, *Decline and Fall*, 2:544–45.

58. Davidson, *A Public Faith*, 121.

and the "righteousness" and miracles attributed to Damasus made him a saint to be adored. However, the accomplishments and administrations of Damasus brought about most of the issues which the sixteenth-century Reformers so vehemently saw as "idolatries" and anti-Christian. Those accomplishments of Damasus included:

1. "The practice of commemorating the saints in the liturgy of the church was extended."[59]

2. The practice of drawing "special attention to the apostolic origins of the Roman see,"[60] especially the elevation of Rome as being the see of Peter, owes to his era, as well as the connection to the relics of Peter's death. His promotion included the denial of the authority of councils to determine the special authority of Rome by the relics of the martyrs, a special authority specifically pagan rather than conciliar.

3. He usurped the jurisdiction of Constantinople by appointing a bishop in Thessalonica and establishing an authoritative foothold in the East (against the canons of Nicaea).

4. He promoted and demanded the veneration of Mary and strong-armed the councils to elevate her as *Theotokos*, "Mother of God."

Jerome was a devoted follower of Origen and an allegorist in the sophistic sense. But upon Origen's fall from church favor, when theologians became convinced that most of his theology was the backbone of Arianism, he switched to become a critic. However, Jerome only castigated Origen concerning his sophistry, because it was Origen's allegorical methodology that Jerome used as a basis for what became the Catholic allegorical method.

Jerome became an opponent to Ambrose, the West's true Nicene and Homoousian scholar. He soon claimed that Ambrose lacked "originality" and had "poor style in his doctrinal and exegetical works."[61] Jerome also attacked others who opposed his purposes. He became the promoter of priestly celibacy and yet was the secretary and participator in the opulent and immoral behavior of his bishop, Damasus. F. F. Bruce suggests that

---

59. Ibid., 120.

60. Ibid.

61. Ibid., 130.

the best thing that ever happened to the church of Rome is that Jerome never became bishop.[62] Paul in his First Epistle to Timothy writes,

> Now the Spirit explicitly says that in latter times some will fall away *[or, apostatize]* from the faith, paying attention to deceitful spirits and teachings of demons, in hypocrisy *[or, insincerity]* of liars, having been seared in their own conscience, forbidding to be marrying, *[commanding]* to be abstaining from foods which God created for receiving with thanksgiving by the *[ones who are]* faithful and have acknowledged the truth. Because every*[thing]* created by God *[is]* good, and nothing *[is to be]* rejected, *[if]* being received with thanksgiving. (1 Tim 4:1–4)

I suppose one can say that Paul prophetically identified Jerome and Damasus as those who "will fall away from the faith," because the two specifically led Rome to priestly celibacy and food ordinances that became the trademark of Rome and the indicator of an apostate church. Yet they did not practice the same. If Jerome opposed Ambrose's orthodoxy, was he not opposing the Nicene position of *homoousios*? Ambrose was the disciple of Athanasius and one of the only Western theologians to hold that position during the reign of the Arian emperor Constantius. But Jerome held strong sway on everything Roman because of his *Vulgata*. The future of orthodoxy in the West was held by the authority of an edited version of the old Italics and Latin texts, which Erasmus in the sixteenth century deemed as unworthy to be used as toilet paper.[63] In his *Novum Instrumentum omne, diligenter ab Erasmo Rot: Recognitum et Emendatum*, a parallel Greek New Testament and Latin translation, he identified over 600 major errors in the Vulgate that produced "grievous and detrimental doctrines to Christianity."[64] I can't say enough about the damage that the Latin Vulgate has caused the Western church.

GENERATION AFTER GENERATION OF REFORMERS

The patriarch Damasus and his secretary, Jerome, started the Roman church toward a millennium of heterdoxical teachings that separated biblical orthodoxy from historical orthodoxy. The future of Rome, through the machinations of the popes, was sold the doctrines of papal authority

62. Bruce, *The Canon of Scripture*, 99.
63. Coogan, *Erasmus, Lee, and the Correction of the Vulgate*, 48.
64. Ibid.

and infallibility over and above the canon of Scripture. Rome would certainly contend that the authority and infallibility of the see of Peter came prior to the Council of Chalcedon's canonization of the twenty-seven books that comprise the New Testament. Thus, church history, according to Rome, would be written and invented by those who promoted the popes to gods, and the doctrines of their imaginations to canon law and Scripture. But it cannot be said that the true Head of the Church was silent through these ages, because generation after generation saw movements of reformation. Just to mention a few: Priscillian wrote letters to Damasus encouraging the Roman church to return to the Scripture.[65] Two of the fathers had opposed Jerome and Damasus in regard to their position on celibacy: Justinian, who produced an explosive opposition to celibacy and fasting, and Vigiliantius, who dedicated several works to expose the falsehood of devotion to the saints and relics.[66]

JEROME'S CATHOLIC ALLEGORICAL METHOD

Jerome utilized the allegorical method of Origen and sent it to Rome in the guise of literalism. Through the sophistic methodology and his translation of the "Greek" texts, he was able to promote celibacy for the clergy of Rome and the West. He translated Scripture in such a way that in the Vulgate, 1 Corinthians 7 is a celibacy chapter. Yet how is it that Paul should encourage celibacy to the Corinthian church when Clement of Rome stated emphatically that Paul was married and that his wife resided in Philippi while he was on his missionary journeys? How is it that Paul was the encourager of celibacy when he was the writer of the Epistle to Timothy in which he attributes forced celibacy to the work of anti-Christ? In it we read, "now the Spirit speaketh expressly, that in the latter times some shall depart from the faith, giving heed to seducing spirits, and doctrines of devils; speaking lies in hypocrisy; having their conscience seared with a hot iron; forbidding to marry, [and commanding] to abstain from

---

65. Priscillian was the Bishop of Avila who was sentenced by the strong arms of Hygenius, bishop of Cordoba, and Hydacius, bishop of Merida, as a Sabellian, an Arian, a Manichaean, an occultist, and a sorcerer, and anything else that could have contrived his demise and anathema. He was executed in 385 CE with many of his followers (possibly as many as 7,000). Damasus condemned the action, but these two bishops were Damasus's lieutenants, and Gratian was the Western emperor who certainly was subjecting himself to the pontiff's suggestion (Bruce, *Advance of Christianity*, 325).

66. Davidson, *A Public Faith*, 190.

meats, which God hath created to be received with thanksgiving of them which believe and know the truth" (1 Tim 4:1–3 KJV).

The skeptic is reminded that Clement of Rome was mentioned in Paul's Epistle to the Philippians (Phil 4:3) in the same context in which he sends a greeting to his *gnēsei syzyge*, which means his "legally bound wife." Those who oppose this translation have swallowed the sophistry of Rome and its impact on the King James Version of the Bible and supposed that the vocative in Greek is gender specific, which it is not. Eusebius quotes this same Clement in writing, "or will they reject even the apostles? . . . while Paul himself does not hesitate in one of his letters to address his wife, whom he did not take around with him in order to facilitate his ministry."[67]

THE DUMBING DOWN OF THEOLOGY IN THE LATIN WEST

One might conclude by the christological debates in the late fourth to mid-fifth century that the detail of explanation employed by the mighty men of theology would ultimately lead to their undoing. The more words used to describe a Word-flesh Christology (Alexandria) or a Word-man Christology (Antioch) would be used as a political tool for the destruction of the theologian making such an assertion. There appeared to be a war for supremacy. Any champion who cared to join the games could find some point in order to un-horse his opponent. The victors were those who bet on the outcome and said very little. The Council of Ephesus did much to destroy any form of theological dialogue between Alexandria and Antioch. At the insistence of Cyril, Nestorius was placed into his custody and consequentially mistreated until Nestorius was dead. John of Antioch acquiesced in fear of the same treatment, while Cyril held the emperor under duress.

But it was Rome who gained the political power, and Celestine presented his trump suit by condemning any bishop from the West who would venture to participate in the Council at Ephesus and insisting that any appeals could come to his attention from any province or jurisdiction within the realm. Such an action drove the wedge between Rome and Carthage deeper. But most of the Western bishops were in compliance, and the outcome put Rome in the Western Latin driver's seat for all doctrinal and theological discussions.

67. Maier, *Eusebius*, 118.

Below is a table of the bishops of Rome as presented by the Vatican; it does not include the extensive list of the anti-popes.

Roman Bishops

Peter	42–67
Linus	67–79
Anacletus	79–92
Clement I	92–101
Evaristus	101–105
Alexander I	105–115
Sixtus I	115–125
Telesphorus	125–136
Hyginis	136–140
Pius I	140–155
Anicetus	155–166
Soter	166–175
Eleutherius	175–189
Victor I	189–199
Zephyrinus	199–217
Callistus I	217–222
Urban I	222–230
Pontian	230–235
Anterius	235–236
Fabian	236–250
Cornelius	251–253
Lucius I	253–254
Stephen I	254–257

Sixtus II	257–258
Dionysius	259–268
Felix I	269–274
Eutychian	275–283
Gaius/Caius	283–296
Marcellinus	296–304
Marcellus I	308–309
Eusebius	309
Miltiades	311–314
Sylvester I	314–335
Mark	336
Julius I	337–352
Liberius	352–366
Damasus I	366–384
Siricius	384–399
Anastasius I	399–401
Innocent I	401–417
Zosimus	417–418
Bonaface I	418–422
Celestine I	422–432
Sixtus III	432–440
Leo I	440–461
Hilary	461–468
Simplicius	468–483
Felix III/II	483–492
Gelasius I	492–496

Anastasius II	496–498
Symmachus	498–514
Hormisdas	514–523
John I	523–526
Felix IV/III	526–530
Bonaface II	530–532
John II	533–535
Agapitus I	535–536
Silverius	536–537
Vigilius	537–555
Pelagius I	556–561
John III	561–574
Benedict I	575–579
Pelagius II	579–590
Gregory I	590–604

5

Hellenism and the Gospel of Alexandria

THE GOSPEL TO ALEXANDRIA

INITIALLY THE GOSPEL WENT south by an unlikely candidate, the Ethiopian eunuch found in Acts 8. It is more likely, however, that the gospel was carried to Alexandria through the Hellenistic Jews attending the Passover at the time of Jesus's crucifixion in 33 CE. The Jewish Hellenist Philo could have been on the scene of Christ's passion as well as the day of Pentecost when the Holy Spirit made his testimony known through the church with power. Philo certainly influenced in many ways the Hellenistic Jewish philosophy that permeated the early Jewish Christians, but could the church also have had an influence on the philosopher? Ferguson notes that several key features of John's gospel also appear earlier in Philo's works. For example, "Philo was a Jew of the Diaspora and his use of *Logos* is prominent and extensive."[1] He also suggests that "the interpretation of the manna in the wilderness in John 6 has points of contact with interpretations found in Philo."[2] To think that John's use of *logos* and his Logos theology was driven by Philo is a little farfetched. It is more likely that Philo just understood the Hellenistic use of the word *logos*. After all, Philo was an Alexandrian Jew and thoroughly encamped in the Platonic school of thought.

Some have suggested that the writer of Hebrews gave particular attention to the philosophies of Philo, but Ferguson suggests that although the evidence is there, he still was only reflecting current Jewish Hellenistic thought and not necessarily drawing anything specific from Philo in his

---

1. Ferguson, *Backgrounds of Early Christianity*, 482.
2. Ibid.

Epistle to the Hebrews.[3] Be that as it may, I believe the reverse took place: that the influence from the early church went actively toward Philo, and some of his particular Hellenistic Jewish notions showed up first in the Hellenistic Jewish Christians by default. For instance, he made some interpretations of the Old Testament that appear to be parallel to those of the Hellenistic Jewish Christian Stephen. Philo, like Stephen, does not give mercy to the Jews where faith is concerned. To be Jewish, in God's economy, is to be of faith. Those who were not of faith and racially Hebrew were not Jews, such as the Cainites. In such matters Philo brought forward an understanding of Old Testament interpretation that pitted the "physical" against the "spiritual." In regard to the parallels that seem to show up between Paul and Philo, Ferguson suggests, "both men fished in the same pool."[4] Was Philo the only one on earth using allegory to understand some points of the Old Testament? The difference in style between Philo and Paul is that Paul stated plainly his allegorical approach so that he would not cast "Plato's shadows" over the church. This also marked the difference between Antioch's and Alexandria's hermeneutics and theology in the middle of the first century and ultimately into the medieval age.

Paul established the Antioch church with a balanced hermeneutic that had its Old Testament understanding in the history of the Jews and the history of God's revelation to them concerning the salvation that was also given to the Gentiles. Philo established the Alexandrian church on an allegorical approach that pitted the history of the Jews and the revelation against a spiritually higher understanding that was to be most sought after. The difference initially in the two founders was style. Philo did not ignore the literal, but never differentiated between the two. Paul was plainly to be understood, whereas Philo was esoteric and preferred to be obscure and was often confusing. In addition, Paul's apostolic authority contrasted with Philo's lack of apostolic authority contributed to the war of the schools in a later century. Philo was an ascetic, while Paul taught that asceticism had no impact on fleshly indulgences. Philo, in the *Contemplative Life*, implied that those who abstained from the flesh of animals had more ability to contemplate and answer higher and pressing questions concerning the Scriptures.[5] "You are what you eat." Paul however, argued that abstinence

---

3. Ibid.

4. Ibid.

5. Philo *The Contemplative Life* 10.75F (Colson trans., 159).

and asceticism was of no value against fleshly indulgence in his letter to the Colossians (Col 2:22–23).

Philo's contribution to hermeneutical rules is evident in the Alexandrian school. He promoted the understanding of Scripture itself as being the key to literal or allegorical interpretation. He initiated a rubric for determining the acceptability of a certain passage being understood both literally and allegorically or only allegorically. Philo persisted in declaring that all of Scripture is to be understood allegorically, but there are three reasons for abandoning the literal interpretation altogether:

1. "if a statement says anything unworthy about God" and

2. "if a statement is contradictory with any other statement or in any other way presents us with difficulty" and

3. "if the record itself is allegorical in nature."[6]

However, the bulk of Philo's exegetical works are not literally understood but allegorically interpreted, as Goppelt writes, "in many passages he excludes the literal meaning, but never the allegorical."[7] Philo in *The Contemplative Life* states, "But the exegesis of the Temple Scriptures are according to the hidden meaning in allegories."[8] Philo's allegorical methodology firmly founded the basis for all Alexandrian exegesis.

Philo held to the view that the "Law" was not a historical account but was a higher moral and spiritual tool of learning providing societies with a godly basis for intellect and rhetoric. He taught that the "Temple Scriptures" were never to be understood historically, and any historical reference is inconsequential to the text. He also taught that plural allegories existed, as one passage conveyed many higher meanings. The pluralistic approach to the Old Testament left the Hellenistic methodology of interpretation literally to be in the eye of the beholder, for there was no provision given by Philo that the interpreter could be found in error in the first place. Philo's approach to hermeneutics left Egypt with an untenable position in theology. The theology and anthropology deduced from the Bible was often "fantastic and absurd."[9] The Rule of Faith was lost

---

6. Ramm, *Protestant Biblical Interpretation*, 27.

7. Goppelt, *Typos*, 49.

8. Philo *Contemplative Life* 10:78, author translation. αἱ δε ἐξηγήσεις τῶν εἱρων γράμματῶν γίνονται δι ὑποινοιων ἕν ἀλλήγιαις.

9. Ramm, *Protestant Biblical Interpretation*, 28.

when Philo's methodology extended to the New Testament because it was no longer necessary to link it to eyewitnesses, as we will see below.

CLEMENT AND HIS ALEXANDRIAN SCHOOL

The first official Christian school of hermeneutics in the south appears in Alexandria and was founded by the early church father Clement, who was a Platonic Hellenist also influenced by Philo. In addition to the rules of allegory established by Philo, Clement saw the scriptural meaning driven by writing type or genre. He recognized five different approaches loosely based on literary type. The historical approach determined that a passage was to be understood as an event in history. The doctrinal approach sought to understand the obvious and apparent "moral, religious and theological teachings."[10] The prophetic method sought to understand Scripture in its "predictive prophecy and typology."[11] In the philosophical approach the Hellenistic philosophies were prevalent, especially Stoicism, which was the preferred school of thought of Clement as well as Philo. The mystical approach understood the Scriptures in truths expressed through symbolism and had every authority in all Scripture. The mystical sense of scriptural interpretation promoted numerology and severe asceticism for it viewed the interpretive methodology in layered levels from the physical (the low form) to the spiritual (the high form). One of the chief issues of Clement's hermeneutic was that by misleading the church regarding high and low forms of biblical interpretation, the church became unaccustomed to critical thinking about the Scriptures. The church of Alexandria did not know when to shut down allegorism, it could not discern when the method was inappropriate. This led to the further expansion of the allegorical methodology. Soon Clement's disciples were fully engaged in all forms of speculative mysticism. One particular disciple was Origen, who argued that all Scripture, including the New Testament, had a higher understanding that was obtained through allegorical methods and superceded any form of literal interpretation.

10. Ibid., 31.

11. Ibid.

ORIGEN AND THE INSTITUTIONAL ALLEGORICAL METHOD

Origen wrote, "He who wishes to take scripture literally had better join the Jews rather than the Christians."[12] I am sure that Paul would argue with Origen on this point. Paul included the historical developments of the ages as all bringing to fruition the salvation to be revealed in Jesus Christ, whereas Origen removed literal historical methodology from that revelation and supposed that the hidden portion of Scripture was instrumental in revealing salvation to man apart from the events of Scripture. All history according to Origen was allegorical and typological. This is certainly true only where the grammar and history can support it. Origen stated regarding his understanding of revelatory, that is, spiritual, interpretation:

> that the Scriptures were written by the Spirit of God, and have a meaning, not such only as is apparent at first sight, but also another, which escapes the notice of most. For those (words) which are written are the forms of certain mysteries, and the images of divine things. Respecting which there is one opinion throughout the whole Church, that the whole law is indeed spiritual; but that the spiritual meaning which the law conveys is not known to all, but to those only on whom the grace of the Holy Spirit is bestowed in the word of wisdom and knowledge.[13]

By applying this methodology to the New Testament writings he removed himself from the apostolic mainstream church and came to untenable and ludicrous applications. One such application was Origen's understanding of piety to such an extreme that to maintain his celibacy he castrated himself.[14] His extreme positions hindered him from being truly the defining source of orthodoxy for future generations of Christians.

In response to the mere fact that Origen's writing can be described as Platonistic, one should recognize that the foundation of Plato and his philosophical school was the only Hellenistic and theistic pattern available to the church in the third century that the church could embrace without difficulty.[15] That was certainly true in Alexandria. Origen was criticized by Libanius of Antioch, the tutor and advisor of Julian the Apostate, as the true philosopher who in a moment of insanity turned to Christianity.

---

12. Quoted in Wallace-Hadrill, *Christian Antioch*, 32.

13. Origen *de Principiis* (Crombie trans., 355–56).

14. "Origen of Alexandria."

15. von Balthasar, *Origen, Spirit and Fire*, xiv.

Because he was one of the finest rhetoricians of his day, the church in his time embraced him as their champion. The thought of the time, especially in Alexandria, was that if you were the enemy of my enemies then you were a true ally, in both faith and doctrine. His writings gained him notoriety, and the church of Alexandria was willing to ride its wave. Through the brilliance of Origen, the southern Christian church distinguished itself apart from the synagogue and distanced itself through his teaching.

Origen's legacy, even though it provided for much of the catholic church's apologetic and polemic against Judaism, also included the foundations for doctrinal disparity that plagued Alexandria and created all sorts of violence in subsequent generations. In his treatment *de Principiis*, Origen departed from the Logos theology of John, or at least confused the distinction of economy and actuality of the Godhead in *tritis hyposteiseis*. His treatment of *tritoi theoi*, "three Gods," provided some points of explanation and ammunition for the Ebionites, the Docetists, and other groups who had denied the full deity of the Son of God. Nevertheless, Origen can in no way be classified with them. If we must categorize the doctrines of Origen, we can simply state that Origen could be considered the father of Arianism. After all is said, Origen's tritheistic doctrine was again only a distorted reaction against the modal Monarchianism of his day.

Without being a Gnostic, Origen indeed explored the depths of the mystery religion and incorporated its predisposition to exclusionism. His emphatic dogma concerning the spiritual nature of Scripture separated the church and mankind into three classes, as defined by Valentinus and the Gnostics: the *heulikoi*, "fleshly," the *psychikoi*, "soulful," and the *pneumatikoi*, "spiritual." Origen, however, was less likely to consider the three classes as cast in stone, and more likely to understand these as growth stages in the Christian life.

Origen's understanding of Logos theology further removes him from orthodoxy. Origen's Christology perceived Christ as preexistent through the prophecies of the Word, which was eternal, but without any appearance or Christophany prior to his incarnation, excepting his part in creation as being the "firstborn of all creation."

> All who believe and are assured that grace and truth were obtained through Jesus Christ, and who know Christ to be the truth, agreeably to His own declaration, "I am the truth" (John 14:6), derive the knowledge which incites men to a good and happy life from no other source than from the very words and teaching of Christ.

And by the words of Christ we do not mean those only which He spake when He became man and tabernacled in the flesh; for before that time, Christ, the Word of God, was in Moses and the prophets. For without the Word of God, how could they have been able to prophesy of Christ? And were it not our purpose to confine the present treatise within the limits of all attainable brevity, it would not be difficult to show, in proof of this statement, out of the Holy Scriptures, how Moses or the prophets both spake and performed all they did through being filled with the Spirit of Christ. And therefore I think it sufficient to quote this one testimony of Paul from the Epistle to the Hebrews 1 in which he says: "By faith Moses, when he was come to years, refused to be called the son of Pharaoh's daughter; choosing rather to suffer affliction with the people of God, than to enjoy the pleasures of sin for a season; esteeming the reproach of Christ greater riches than the treasures of the Egyptians."[16]

Origen believed not only in the subordination of Christ to the Father by his incarnation, but also from the creation, as he states "That Jesus Christ Himself, who came (into the world), was born of the Father before all creatures; that, after He had been the servant of the Father in the creation of all things—'For by Him were all things made' (John 1:3)—He in the last times, divesting Himself (of His glory), became a man, and was incarnate although God, and while made a man remained the God which He was."[17] Origen thought that Christ (the Son) was immutable in his existence and was a created being. However, he remained unchanged in nature before the incarnation, during the incarnation, and after the incarnation. Origen's concept of γένης or "begotten" was specifically viewed in Hellenistic terms as being made, but not in Hebrew terms as being declared to be the Son of the Father.

HYPOSTASIS AND SUBSTANTIA ARE THE SAME

"If, then, it is once rightly understood that the only-begotten Son of God is His wisdom hypostatically existing, I know not whether our curiosity ought to advance beyond this, or entertain any suspicion that that ὑπόστασις or substantia contains anything of a bodily nature, since

---

16. Origen de Principiis (Crombie trans., 353).

17. Ibid., (Crombie trans., 240).

everything that is corporeal is distinguished either by form, or colour, or magnitude."[18]

Origen also believed that there was a time when the Son was not in existence, as he interprets the Logos passage of John. Instead of defining Logos by Tertullian's standard (as explained in chapter 6 of this book). Origen did not see wisdom as beginning in rational thought and reason, and argued that the Father had assigned Logos to the Son upon his creation as the Father's own wisdom or "Word." Thus, stating that Wisdom being the beginning of the ways of God, and was created, and that the Word (*Logos*) is wisdom, therefore it was created. By making such an assumption of John's *Logos* theology, Origen implied that God had no wisdom before He "created" the Son.

> Now, in the same way in which we have understood that Wisdom was the beginning of the ways of God, and is said to be created, forming beforehand and containing within herself the species and beginnings of all creatures, must we understand her to be the Word of God, because of her disclosing to all other beings, i.e., to universal creation, the nature of the mysteries and secrets which are contained within the divine wisdom; and on this account she is called the Word, because she is, as it were, the interpreter of the secrets of the mind. And therefore that language which is found in the *Acts of Paul*, where it is said that "here is the Word a living being," appears to me to be rightly used. John, however, with more sublimity and propriety, says in the beginning of his Gospel, when defining God by a special definition to be the Word, "And God was the Word and this was in the beginning with God." Let him, then, who assigns a beginning to the Word or Wisdom of God, take care that he be not guilty of impiety against the unbegotten Father Himself.[19]

Origen's point was simply that the Son was assigned the Father's wisdom upon the Father's creation of the Son, and therefore the subjected Son in no way demeans the Father, because he is not the Father but was created by him.

According to Origen, the Son had no corporeal body and was not corporeal, for Origen misconstrued Paul, believing that "Christ was the

---

18. Ibid., (Crombie trans., 246).
19. Ibid., (Crombie trans., 246).

invisible image of the invisible God" rather than the visible image of the invisible God (1 Cor 1:15):

> Let us now see how we are to understand the expression "invisible image," that we may in this way perceive how God is rightly called the Father of His Son; and let us, in the first place, draw our conclusions from what are customarily called images among men. That is sometimes called an image which is painted or sculptured on some material substance, such as wood or stone; and sometimes a child is called the image of his parent, when the features of the child in no respect belie their resemblance to the father. But the image of the Son of God, of whom we are now speaking, may be compared to the second of the above examples, even in respect of this, that He is the invisible image of the invisible God, in the same manner as we say, according to the sacred history, that the image of Adam is his son Seth. The words are, "And Adam begat Seth in his own likeness, and after his own image" (Gen 5:3). Now this image contains the unity of nature and substance belonging to Father and Son. For if the Son do, in like manner, all those things which the Father doth, then, in virtue of the Son doing all things like the Father, is the image of the Father formed in the Son, who is born of Him, like an act of His will proceeding from the mind.[20]

These arguments show that Origen held that there was a time when the Son was not.

THE DISCORD OF ORIGEN WITH THE NICENE THEOLOGY

At the end of the Nicene Creed is a list of what are called anathemas. Because the focus of the anathemas in 325 was levied against the Arian heresy they were written with specific connections to the elements in the heresy that were opposed to the position of the New Testament Scriptures and the apostles who wrote them. Care was taken not to include any doctrine that alluded to the writings that by consensus the body of Christians said were pseudepigraphical and deemed forgeries with known apostolic names falsely attached. Those anathemas read as follows:

> And those who say "there once was when he was not", and "before he was begotten he was not", and that he came to be from things that were not, or from another hypostasis [Gr. *hypostaseōs*] or substance [Gr. *ousias*, Lat. *substantia*], affirming that the Son of God

20. Ibid. (Crombie trans., 247).

is subject to change or alteration these the catholic and apostolic church *anathematises*.[21]

In reviewing the writings of Origen we find that Origen held many of the beliefs concerning the Son of God to which Arius ascribed. But Origen lived in a simpler time with simpler doctrinal rubrics. To maintain orthodoxy at the time of Origen one needed only to oppose certain heretical groups such as Valentinians, Marcionites, Ebionites. These all arose out of extreme Judaism or extreme Hellenism applied to the gospel. The legalization of the Christian church made the rubric much more complex. Heresy was viewed not on the extreme but on the subtlety. If a teacher taught a doctrine or explained the economy and character of God a certain way, how did that fit with the entirety of the scriptural text, and ultimately did it promote something false about God? Origen, even though dead, found his doctrine in this dilemma. Most of the fathers of the church during his own day responded well to Origen's brilliance in exposing the Gnostics, Ebionites, and Docetists, but in the time of Constantine the church was asking the critical questions about the Christ, the incarnation, the ministry of Christ to the church, and his relationship to the Father. These modern theologians found in Origen the beginnings of the problems of Arius's teachings, namely, his subjectionist position of the Christ, his tritheistic explanation of the trinitas, his insistence that the Father and the Son are not of the same substance, but are one only in power and agreement, and that the Son was created. When reviewing what was objectionable about the violent movement in Alexandria, they found Origen to be of the same ilk with Arius, and posthumously declared his writings to be heresy. In Alexandria the violence of the party of Arius was the initial revelation of the problem for the greater orthodox church. This problem divided the church into violent schismatic groups, and in Constantine's judgment jeopardized the security of the newly formed Christian empire.

To illustrate the connection between Arius and Origen made by the church at large, canon one of the Council at Nicaea stated,

> If anyone in sickness has undergone surgery at the hands of physicians or has been castrated by barbarians, let him remain among the clergy. But if anyone in good heath has castrated himself, if he is enrolled among the clergy he should be suspended, and in future no such man should be promoted. But, as it is evident that this

---

21. Nicene Creed of 325.

refers to those who are responsible for the condition and presume to castrate themselves, so too if any have been made eunuchs by barbarians or by their masters, but have been found most worthy (*dignissimi*), the canon (*regula*) admits such men to the clergy.[22]

In the days of Origen the bishop Demetrius of Alexandria would not receive him for ordination because of his hideous act of mutilation, and it also appears that this issue tells of the condemnation of not only Origen's act but also his doctrine—a condemnation aimed at Arius. It seems that at the time of Nicaea Arius's borrowed doctrine and Origen's radical lifestyle were considered contrary to the faith of the apostles and the Scriptures. Or could it be that Arius may have castrated himself also to mimic his ancient doctrinal source, or that within the Arian party the practice became prevalent?

PRIOR TO NICAEA

Origen's theology had a lasting impact on the school of Alexandria, continuing through his disciples Heraclas, Dionysius, Theognotis, and later Pierius. Pierius developed the Origen model even more by stating that the Father and Son were "οὐσίαι," "beings."[23] Pierius's teaching expounded on the two beings that were not of the same substance or nature but united by agreement, power and shared authority. Pierius was the headmaster of the school when Arius started to excel in Christian philosophy. Of Pierius, Jerome states that he taught with "such elegance of language" that he was called "Origen Junior."[24] But in the mix of archbishops in Alexandria came one from Lybia and a disciple of Theonas whose name was Peter.[25] Peter held to a form of orthodoxy that might not be Nicene in fullness, yet he was able to see something amiss in the theology and activity of Arius. Specifically, Arius had supported the ministry of Meletius and had urged the bishop to withdraw his earlier excommunication of the tyrannical bishop. The arrogance in which Arius approached the bishop only brought his own excommunication also.

22. Pennington, "A Short History of Canon Law," Nicaea canon 1.

23. Kelly, *Early Christian Doctrines*, 133.

24. Jerome *De viris illustribus* 76 (Richardson trans.).

25. Anastasius the Librarian *The Genuine Acts of Peter, Bishop of Alexandria and Martyr.*

After the martyrdom of Peter the Bishop during the third wave of Diocletian's persecution, Arius recanted so that he could be reinstated during the six-month rule of Achillas, who promoted Arius to the priesthood and eldership. But when Achillas died, he was replaced by Alexander of Antioch.

Alexander heard the disputation between Arius and the orthodox clergy. There was a problem when each party believed that they had carried the day. As a result Arius became more aggressive and repugnant, and led his party into a battle of low blows. Alexander then looked into the situation as the newly appointed archbishop and discovered that Achillas and Arius had entered into a conspiracy to supplant the orthodox clergy with violence and malice, just as Colluthus had done before him, and to lead the Alexandrian see away from the truth of the *trinitas* and the Logos theology.[26]

Alexander at this juncture saw that the two groups had come to an impasse, and that there was no program of action for the reconciliation of the Arian party, because Arius had "brought into question all pious and apostolic doctrine, after the manner of the Jews [Ebionites]."[27] Therefore, he deposed the elders—Arius, Aithalas, Achiles, Carpones, Sarmates—and the deacons: Euzoius, Macarius, Julias, Menas, and Helladius. All of these persons held that Christ was made from nonsubstance, that there was a time when the Son did not exist, and that free will is preeminent and one is able to choose virtue or evil, because the soul or mind of men was not fallen.[28]

Eusebius of Nicomedia attempted to intervene on behalf of the wayward clerics and tried desperately to convince Alexander to reverse his deposition. Having failed that, he tried to compel the reversal of the decision by raising commotion about Alexander's orthodoxy. With the help of the entourage of deposed clergy from Alexandria, he accused Alexander of being a Sabellianist.[29] Having failed there, Eusebius of Nicomedia supported the Arian group's doctrine, and sent them monetary and manpower support to raise disputations in the church of Alexandria. These disputations became more intense and violent until Constantine sought to bring

26. Alexander, *Letter to the Bishop of Constantinople* (Hawkins trans., 291).

27. Ibid.

28. Sozomen *Ecclesiasticus* (Hartranft trans., 251–52).

29. Ibid.

peace. He sent letters to both parties and then called for the Council of Nicaea, with 318 bishops attending.

But why did Constantine call for the council? After all wasn't this just a regional dispute? Primarily, Constantine was responsible as emperor to keep the Pax Romana, but Alexandria was always a problem in the history of the emperors. Therefore, throughout his reign Constantine's dealings with Alexandria were characterized by mistrust and suspicion. Before his conversion Constantine grew up in the court of Diocletian in the East. His schooling was that of a prince, of which he took the utmost advantage. Later that education and his familiarity with the records of the East and of Rome were instrumental in understanding his empire, negotiating, deciding, and implementing the best plans to keep the Pax Romana. Searching the archives, Constantine may have run across the letter of Hadrian to Phlegan that was disparaging to all Christian leaders in Egypt, as he remarks that he is,

> well acquainted with the Egyptians as frivolous and avid for novelties: "Here those who worship Serapis are [at the same time] Christians, and those who call themselves bishops of Christ are also devotees of Serapis. Here there is no synagogue leader of the Jews, no Samaritan, no Christian presbyter who is not also an astrologer, a haruspex, and an aliptes."[30]

This and many other evidences had convinced Constantine of the need to send Alexander from Antioch to Alexandria earlier. He may have deduced that all the volatile behavior in Alexandria was caused by the radically superstitious Egyptian majority that sought to defend their pagan thoughts with the manipulation of Scripture.[31]

After the Council of Nicaea, the aging Alexander took the back seat to his promising deacon Athanasius. It was observed throughout the Christian leadership at the council that Athanasius had shined and represented the Homoousian party with the utmost skill and confidence. Even Constantine was satisfied with the young leader. With Alexander's successor at hand, he could decline in peace, knowing that the orthodox position established at Nicaea would be well represented. By early spring

30. Bauer, *Orthodoxy and Heresy in Earliest Christianity*, 64.

31. The problem of the authenticity of the letter of Hadrian is superimposed by the Western Latin veneration of the saints Clement, Origen, and Cyril, all of which are Alexandrian and of the same time or ilk of those rogue leaders of the Egyptian churches.

of 326 CE Alexander had died. But Alexandria was a hard milieu for any bishop, and the party of Arius would not go away. The struggle between the two parties continued, and it was not until 328 CE that the orthodox churches of Alexandria were able to muster the votes and power base to get the Homoousian champion into Alexander's vacated position.

Arius had been exiled to Thrace, but the damage in Alexandria was done. Athanasius received a plethora of accusations and abuse from the party who sought his demise. The intensity of the derision even reached the emperor in the form of indictments sent concerning the impieties and immoralities of Athanasius. It was even reported to Constantine that Athanasius had delayed grain shipments of wheat to the capital in defiance of the emperor. All of these were false of course. Nevertheless, the word was out and the damage done, as there would always be that suspicion in the mind of the population and the emperor himself. Constantine countered with the reinstatement of Arius after Arius had falsified a recantation and an acceptance of the Creed.

Athanasius refused his admittance to his former position as *presbyteros*. Athanasius knew that Arius would return to a mob of his clones that thirsted for his blood. Arius's reinstatement meant the death of Athanasius by assassination and the struggle for any form of orthodox Christianity in Africa. But defiance of the emperor was still defiance of the emperor. In 335 CE Athanasius was deposed and exiled by Constantine to Trier in Europe. It is curious here why Constantine would extricate his champion of orthodoxy unless the moderate Eusebius of Caesarea advised him to do so. But God has a better plan, and his exile brought about orthodoxy in the West, as Ambrose was certainly affected by the ministry of Athanasius through Hilary of Poitiers. Ambrose later became the orthodox mouthpiece for the whole of the West.

THE ARIAN POLITICAL STRUGGLE OF POST-NICENE CHRISTIANITY

Arianism was not dealt a death blow, even though bishops were removed, leaders of the Arian churches were exiled, and Arius's writings destroyed. The Arians learned an important lesson. The focal point of power was empirical and the emperor must be won over. The outcome of the Council of Nicaea made it clear that the church and the state are united, and in a unified empire the emperor was supreme. Most of the bishops who supported the Arian position had signed the Creed with a general and sophistic interpretation of the word ὁμοούσιας. Eusebius of Nicomedia and Theognis of Nicaea signed the Creed but withheld their support of the anathemas that were prescribed against Arian leadership. Hence they were deposed and banished for a time.[32] Theonas and Secundus, who had "refused to sign," accompanied Arius into exile.[33]

The message to the Arian element was clear. The remainder of those who flew under the radar with false testimony and support of the Creed would market their doctrine to the offspring of the emperor, and even the empress. By biding their time they would ultimately be restored to power and revoke the comfort of the orthodox bishops. Constantine was old and his patience was wearing thin when the Pax Romana was at stake. He had made it a criminal act to disagree with the theology of the council and the emperor in truth or in error.[34] Constantine had assumed that the Nicene Creed and the council put an end to all speculation, debate, and theological warring for all time.

Athanasius had reached a similar understanding in that he states that the council was "a true monument and token against every heresy."[35] But his reign as bishop of Alexandria was wracked by controversy and adversity, which included three exiles during the reigns of six different emperors. Athanasius was right about the significance of the Creed, but he could not enforce it unless it was supported from Constantinople. Unfortunately for the church, this reality held for the opposition also after Nicaea, and they attached themselves to the imperial family whenever they could.

After the death of Constantine the atmosphere in Constantinople was changed by the aggressive and influential leaders of the Homoiousian party. Constantius leaned toward the Arians after he was diverted from his openness to Athanasius by the advice of Valens, who had become an important advisor to him and his family. But Constantius did nothing to

---

32. Schaff, *History of the Christian Church*, 3:629.

33. Ibid.

34. Constantine had sent an edict to the churches of Egypt and Ethiopia ascribing divine inspiration to the outcome of the Council and stating that its findings constituted civil law. But that ascription had its down side, as stated above: it became illegal to disagree theologically with the emperor, and it became his duty to enforce it however it suited him.

35. Schaff, *History of the Christian Church*, 3:630.

enforce the civil law as he was inclined to be at peace with all. Constantius supported the notion of flexibility within the church concerning Christ's status as divine.[36] He was advised by Valens to buy the affection and the compliance of peace within the church by providing large amounts of bribes to the orthodox Nicene bishops for retention of their bishoprics for agreeing to do nothing against Homoian and Homoiousian bishops and clergy.

Nothing could be accomplished in Alexandria until the venerable Athanasius was out of the way. But with the wild popularity and the power base that Athanasius possessed, Valens needed to wait for two dominoes to fall. It was imperative that the demise of Athanasius be natural, otherwise violence would erupt in Egypt. Valens also needed the imperial power and authority of Constantinople. Eventually he received both. After the downfall of Julian, the successor Valentinian appointed his brother Valens to rule the East (364 CE). For two years, however, Valens was engaged in securing his empire from the rebellion of Procopius. Until 366 CE he could do nothing until the usurper was removed from the capital. But upon his successful defense of his rule, Valens erupted with resolve. Later, upon Athanasius's death in 373, the Homoousian Peter succeeded him to the bishopric, but the machinations of Valens were already in operation.

RESTORATION OF THE ARIANS UNDER VALENS

Having deposed the orthodox bishops of both Constantinople and Antioch and replacing them with Arians, Valens made a clean sweep by imprisoning Peter and appointed Lucius bishop of Alexandria. He followed the appointment with an edict sent to the governor of Egypt to remove and exile all the leaders who followed or were sympathetic to the Homoousian theology. This brought about violent action against the orthodox groups. According to Socrates,

> the emperor Valens issued an edict commanding that the ortho-
> dox should be persecuted both in Alexandria and in the rest of
> Egypt, depopulation and ruin to an immense extent immediately
> followed: some were dragged before tribunals, others cast into
> prison, and many tortured in various ways, and in fact all sorts

36. Davidson, *A Public Faith*, 54.

of punishments were inflicted upon persons who aimed only at peace and quiet.[37]

Socrates later mentioned that whole populations of orthodox churches were disposed of through martyrdom.

CYRIL, THE ALEXANDRIAN DESPOT
AND THE MONOPHYSITE RISE TO POWER

Gibbon writes, "The name of Cyril of Alexandria is famous in a controversial story, and the title of *saint* is a mark that his opinions and his party have finally prevailed."[38] Cyril's power struggle was a long and bloody one that was full of strife, dissension, and even violence. When Cyril was in the house of his uncle, the archbishop Theophilus, he was raised in the "orthodox lessons of zeal and dominion,"[39] but unfortunately, not in the doctrine that could be classed as biblical orthodoxy. The hermeneutic of Origen he detested; but that of his favorites, Clemens and Dionysius, Athanasius and Basil, he adapted to his own philosophical needs and theological patterns. Theophilus brought him out of the desert of asceticism and monasticism to introduce him to the world of theological and secular politics and placed him in the committee to oppose John Chrysostom. As a result, Cyril became the political strategist that marked the Alexandrian administration for the next two hundred years until the Muslim Arabs reduced the city to mediocrity.

The pragmatic education that Cyril received from his uncle even brought the ecclesiastic to view the death of Theophilus as a benefit for his own personal gain. As Gibbon writes, "The death of Theophilus expanded and realized the hopes of his nephew. The clergy of Alexandria was divided; the soldiers and their general supported the claims of the archdeacon; but a resistless multitude, with voices and with hands, asserted the cause of their favorite; and after a period of thirty-nine years, Cyril was seated on the throne of Athanasius."[40]

Cyril always saw the patriarchate of Alexandria as the driving force of all Africa and the head of ecclesiastical and secular authority second only to the bishop of Rome. "The prize [of the patriarchate] was not un-

37. Socrates Scholasticus, *Church History* (Zenos trans., 109).
38. Gibbon, *Decline and Fall*, 5:15–16.
39. Ibid., 5:15.
40. Ibid.

worthy of his ambition. At a distance from the court, and at the head of an immense capital, the patriarch, as he was now styled, of Alexandria had gradually usurped the state and authority of a civil magistrate."[41] Once enthroned in Alexandria and having won the secular authority of the capital, he was able to strike out toward any of those who might oppose him or even peaceably disagree with him. He took out the Novatians (a peaceful heretical group of sectaries that held that the office of patriarch was not biblical and held an Origenist understanding of subjectionism). He also devoured the peace and properties of the Jewish population of over 40,000. His next focus was the oriental East, and he began to challenge the power of the other Eastern patriarchs. Rather than embrace and acquiesce to the orthodoxy from Antioch and Constantinople, he decided to make Alexandria the primal Eastern see and supported several heterodox cults who strongly opposed the teachings from the school of Antioch. Specifically, he provided sanction for a Monophysite and promoted the doctrine to oppose the patriarchates of Antioch and Constantinople toward his own promotion. This drew the orthodox bishops into the fray. His fellow patriarchs became the enemy, and he launched ecclesiastical wars against Proclus, the disciple of John Chrysostom, and Nestorius of Constantinople, and then John of Antioch.

At the time of the Council of Ephesus, his war strategy combined the might of a standing army[42] with the sway of monetary bribes, and the theory and practice of the dispute. "The fleet which had transported Cyril from Alexandria was laden with the riches of Egypt; and he disembarked a numerous body of mariners, slaves, and fanatics, enlisted with blind obedience under the banner of St. Mark and the mother of God."[43] He won the day at Ephesus with the show of force and usurped the lead of the council itself by overwhelming the bishops who had gathered. Nestorius's party and John of Antioch's party had not arrived, but the proceeds were completed and the canons written by the skilled hand of Cyril. The anathemas waged against Nestorius were added after the signatures of the bishops had been obtained.

Some five days later the contingents of John of Antioch entered the city. "On the fifth day, the triumph was clouded by the arrival and indigna-

41. Ibid.
42. Cyril had entered Ephesus with a military force of over 500 at his disposal.
43. Gibbon, *Decline and Fall*, 5:23.

tion of the Eastern bishops."[44] Candidian, the imperial minister who had suggested proceeding with caution in the earlier days of the council, and who had been ostracized by the sharp rebuke of Cyril and his puppets and put out violently from the court, reported to John immediately upon his arrival. The synod of John and fifty bishops arriving with him was forced to counter the actions of the "monkey trial." So as Gibbon puts it, "with equal haste and violence, the Oriental synod of fifty bishops degraded Cyril and Memnon from their episcopal honors, condemned, in the twelve anathemas, the purest venom of the Apollinarian heresy, and described the Alexandrian primate as a monster, born and educated for the destruction of the church."[45] Violence broke out as Cyril and Memnon, the bishop of Ephesus, barricaded themselves and their contingents within the church, which resembled a siege and not a council. The forces of Candidian's siege soon retreated, but they were molested by the vigorous salvo from the Cyrillian army at their flank. Gibbon goes on to report the outcome of the violence: "they [the Oriental party of bishops] lost their horses, and many of their soldiers were dangerously wounded with clubs and stones."[46]

Theodosius II, having discerned foul play in Ephesus, disavowed the proceedings of the Council. He urged the parties involved to stop the violence immediately and return to their provinces: "God is my witness," said the pious prince, "that I am not the author of this confusion. His providence will discern and punish the guilty. Return to your provinces, and may your private virtues repair the mischief and scandal of your meeting."[47] But Theodosius II was indecisive in the matter because his sister Pulcheria[48] held a heavy hand over her younger brother. Pulcheria was a strong supporter of Cyril, Arianism, the Monophysites, and the cult of the *Theotokos*. Pulcheria, with the assistance of "Dalmatius and Eutyches ... devoted their zeal and fidelity to the cause of Cyril, the worship of Mary, and the unity of Christ."[49] Cyril had also entered triumphantly into Constantinople with his contingent troops and his bag of money, thus winning over the support of Theodosius. The canons stood. The anath-

---

44. Ibid.
45. Ibid., 5:25.
46. Ibid.
47. Ibid., 5:26.
48. Pulcheria had proclaimed herself "empress" in 414 CE.
49. Gibbon, *Decline and Fall*, 5:27.

emas on Nestorius remained, and the exiled Nestorius sought to return to the monastery of his earlier days. Cyril was incensed at such a notion, and with impunity he had Nestorius imprisoned and delivered to his brother's monastery in Egypt where he died under torturous treatment.

The Second Council of Ephesus was opened on August 8, 449 CE. The design was to affirm the position of the church in Alexandria as the dominating one. The Patriarch Dioscorus of Alexandria contrived a plan to remove all orthodox leaders from the East with the help of the Monophysite bishop of Ephesus and the emperor Theodosius II, who had been subverted by the *Theotokos* party. Leo I of Rome closely aligned himself to the Monophysites because he had already joined them in his Monothelite position. The Monophysite and Monothelite positions held rule as a result of the veneration of Mary and the theology of the *Theotokos.* The orthodox position of the dual natures of Christ was backed into the corner and held the minority position. The Council itself sought its own consensus and pushed through its anathemas by the day's power-mongers, Dioscorus and Leo I. Cyril's earlier victories over the oriental orthodoxy of John of Antioch and Nestorius of Constantinople left most of the church patriarchs, including Constantinople, embracing at least the Monophysite doctrine. Eutyches of Constantinople was in full support, and therefore the emperor would not dare disturb the public peace with any opposition.

Ultimately, the brazen move on the part of the Monophysites dis-turbed the balance, and realizing that these powerbrokers had usurped the orthodoxy of Nicaea, Antioch and the bishopric of the orient countered in 451 at the Council of Chalcedon. After the orthodoxy of the Nicene Council was restored with Chalcedon and the Council of Ephesus was revoked, Dioscorus' action became known to the church as the Robber Council of Ephesus. The Monophysites made the mistake of striking too soon, and once done there was no way out for Alexandria except to remove itself from the catholic communion and separate itself in a schismatic group, which later encouraged the Fatimid Muslims in Egypt. Thus the Coptic Church was born, which claims its first pope as Dioscorus. Patriarch Timothy II of Alexandria was the Monophysite leader of Alexandria at the time of Chalcedon and was sent into exile by the council. But the Chalcedonian-appointed bishop Timothy III was murdered, and Timothy II was restored. Timothy II removed Alexandria as a schismatic see and then sorely persecuted the Chalcedonian party.

The die was cast, and the unity of doctrine and love was not to commend itself between the oriental East and Alexandria. From that time on Alexandria alienated itself in the mono-heresies of Monophysitism and Monothelitism. These heretical parties sought dominance in Alexandria by forcefully extracting the orthodox party. Nestorians and later the Chalcedonians were forced out of Jerusalem and Antioch. Looking for redemption from the patriarch of Constantinople and his Chalcedonian orthodoxy, the Monophysite bishops received the Muslim Arabs as deliverers in the seventh century.

Below is a table of the patriarchs of Alexandria, which includes the Monophysite Coptic Church.

Patriarchs of Alexandria[50]

St. Mark I the Evangelist	43–61, d.63
Anianus	61–82
Avilius	83–95
Kedron	96–106
Primus	106–118
Justus	118–129
Eumenes	131–141
Mark II	142–152
Celadion	152–166
Agrippinus	167–178
Julian	178–189
Demetrius	189–232
Heraclas	232–248
St. Dionysius	248–264
Maximus	265–282

50. Square brackets within the table of patriarchs indicate a split bishopric, that is, other bishops while Athanasius was in exile.

Theonas	282–300
St. Peter I	300–311
Achillas	312–313
St. Alexander I	313–328
St. Athanasius I	328–373
[Pistus]	335–337
[Gregory]	340–346
[George]	357–361
[Lucius]	365, 375–378
Peter II	373–380
Timothy I	380–385
Theophilus I leads destruction of the Serapeum, 391	385–412
St. Cyril I	412–444
St. Dioscorus I president of the "Robber Council," Ephesus II, 449, Monophysitism affirmed	444–451, d. 454
St. Proterius	452–457
Timothy/Timotheos	457–460
II Eluros	475–477

Coptic Patriarchs of Alexandria

Petros III Monge	477, 482–489
Athanasios II Keletes	489–496
Yoannis I	496–505
Yoannis II	505–516
Dioscoros II	516–517
Timotheos III	517–535

6

Constantinople, the New Roman Christian Empire

CONSTANTINOPLE: THE FOCUS TOWARD NICAEA AND A CHRISTIAN EMPIRE

CONSTANTINOPLE HAD ITS ORIGIN in 326 at the design and plans of Constantine. Although the city preexisted as Byzantium for almost 600 years, it had little significance, and should be considered a village and not a city before Constantine's plans to make it the center of the Christian Roman Empire. But prior to these plans, Constantine's interest in the East was prompted by the disregard of Licinius to the Milan policy and the treaty that the two signed. Rudimentary analysis suggests that what prompted Constantine to embark on a war against his ally was the anti-Christian pogrom of Licinius. However, documents suggest that Licinius favored the Arian bishops over the orthodox bishops. In a letter of condemnation and deposition of Eusebius of Nicomedia, Constantine suggested that the persecution under Licinius was not pagan against Christian, but Arian Christian against Orthodox Christian. Constantine wrote,

> Who, I beg of you, is the person who taught this to a guileless people? Eusebius to be sure the participator in the tyrant's savagery (concerning the persecution of Licinius). For that he was constantly a client of the tyrant can be understood from many circumstances. The killing of bishops—I mean true bishops—bears witness to this, the most relentless persecution of Christians proclaims it explicitly.[1]

His letter also stated that Eusebius had come to spy on Constantine, disguised as a clerical entourage, and reported back to Licinius during the siege of Byzantium. We can make several observations from his letter:

1. Frend, "The Conduct and Exile of Eusebius of Nicomedia," in *New Eusebius*, 351.

1. Licinius had broken the treaty by killing many orthodox bishops and placed his Arian ones in those positions left vacant by the murders, making most of Asia pro-Arian.

2. There were plots within even Constantine's own family to destroy the monarch.[2]

3. Constantine's war was won at Byzantium, the site of the final battle against Licinius, and Constantine's plan for Constantinople was to continue the battle from this stronghold, taking it into the Arian-controlled bishoprics.

Constantine returned to Rome in 326 CE for the last time. His purpose was deliberate. Immediately, Constantine shut down the prominent position of the city by moving his Western capital to Milan and establishing a palace for himself and the royal family. He deeded the palace of Fausta to the bishop of Rome for a residence; after all, she would no longer need it because she had been executed for having an affair with his son and her stepson, Crispus. The whole event must have taken place on the journey to Rome as Crispus was executed on the road.[3] He started the construction of three major churches in Rome—St. Paul's, St. Peter's, and a large portion of Fausta's palace dedicated as a worship center which Constantine gave to the bishop Sylvester as a residence (known as the Laterine palace)—in hopes that in future generations Rome might abandon the old gods.

Constantine's haste in traveling west so soon after his and Christendom's apparent victory in Nicaea promptly established his dislike for and his abandonment of Roman preeminence in his imperial order. Could it have been because the church in the West did not attend the Council in Nicaea? Several reasons have been suggested for their inattention:

1. Rome was predominantly pagan and worshiped the old Roman gods, and the church in Rome was weak in faith and in strength of numbers.

---

2. Eusebius of Nicomedia was a distant relative to Constantia, Constantine's stepsister and wife of Licinius. Eusebius was also a relative of Julian the Apostate, and raised him for a half dozen years in Nicomedia.

3. Norwich, *Shorter History of the Byzantine Empire*, 11.

2. Those who were leaders in the church of Rome were arrogant and corrupt, just as the pagan Roman bureaucracy had been.

3. The West, unlike Alexandria, Antioch, Ephesus, and Jerusalem, was not accustomed to theological dialogue and viewed Nicaea as an unimportant issue because their abilities in Christian thought and doctrine were rudimentary at best.

Constantine established his capital in the East by building a new city on the site of the ancient Byzantium. By doing so he insured the Roman Empire of life for another millennium. The new city would be established in Christianity and would not have the old pagan baggage that, as Norwich states, was foundational to "Rome, whose republican and pagan traditions could clearly have no place in his new Christian empire."[4] The site of the "New Rome" was the most strategic geography in the entire East, which marked a gateway to control of most of Europe. This change of site for the empire demonstrates the genius of Constantine: The East was the pearl of the empire providing it with over eighty percent of its wealth. Four scenarios demanded the change:

1. The Persian Empire had encroached on the fertile Tigris and Euphrates valleys; a strong presence in Anatolia, Mesopotamia, and Armenia would be imperative for the security of the empire and could be supplied, outfitted, and deployed from Constantinople.

2. The Huns were starting to move west in the steppes and pushed the Goths, Visigoths, Ostrogoths, and Vandals into Thrace and the Balkans. Therefore, a large military presence could be deployed for action from the fortresses planned at and around Constantinople. Control of the two seas (Aegean and Black) could be established with a single navy, while the Bosporus, the Sea of Marmara and the Golden Horn were under the guard of the city itself.

3. The Christian presence was well established in the East and secured by the majority of the population, which made a great foundation for the "New Christian" order.

---

4. Ibid., 12.

4. Rome was indefensible, having been sacked by invaders over three times in the six hundred years prior. The position of "New Rome" (Constantinople) was perfect for constructing a state of the art city that would remain impenetrable for over a thousand years.

His plan included the control of trade in the Mediterranean by building and outfitting a substantial naval force. The fleet that he had used to defeat Licinius in the Dardanelles was largely intact, and building from there the Roman Empire could control the shipping lanes for the entirety of northern Africa, Asia Minor, the Greek states and isles, Italy, Gaul, Thrace, Bulgaria, and Phanagoria. Peace was revoked by the consensus of both emperors:

> Constantine sent Crispus Caesar with a large fleet to take possession of Asia, and on the side of Licinius, Amandus opposed him, likewise with naval forces.... Then Licinius fled to Byzantium; and while his scattered forces were on the way to the city, Licinius closed it, and feeling secure against an attack by sea, planned to meet a siege from the land-side. But Constantine got together a fleet from Thrace. Then Licinius, with his usual lack of consideration, chose Martinianus as his Caesar. But Crispus, with Constantine's fleet, sailed to Callipolis, where in a sea-fight he so utterly defeated Amandus that the latter barely made his escape with the help of the forces which he had left on shore. But Licinius's fleet was in part destroyed and in part captured.[5]

After the Dardanelles in 324 CE, about half of Licinius's fleet was captured and almost 300 triremes were added to Constantine's naval power and over 350 were sunk by the talented young Crispus who had been appointed Megas Doux of the fleet. Unfortunately, the genius of the young admiral was lost by his execution in 326. This navy was not disbanded until 1293, during the reign of Adronicus II.[6]

Constantine from an early age had a sense of destiny or call. During the final persecution of the church at the hands of Diocletian and Galerius in 303, he found himself for "religious reasons" under house arrest at Diocletian's courts in Rome. Fearing for his life, he escaped to his father, Contantius Chlorus, in Bologne, and made plans with him on a military

---

5. Ammianus Marcellinus *Res Geste* (Rolfe trans., 523).

6. Ibid., 331.

expedition into Britannia. Whether this "religious" cause for incarceration was that at this early time Constantine embraced Christianity is unknown, but it is well established that his father Constantius had established a sympathy to the Christians in his region, and that both father and son were known among the "monotheists." Many of the principal officers of Chlorus's regime were known Christians.[7]

Two additional durations of Christian persecution are recorded in the East from Emperor Maximin, who under the guise of toleration drew out the secret groups of the religious sect into the public scrutiny and proceeded to attempt to annihilate them in Asia Minor and Syria, and finally a third persecution under Licinius who had responded to the advice of Eusebius of Nicomedia in removing and killing Orthodox bishops in violation of the agreement made with Constantine regarding the Milan Policy of 313.[8]

Seizing on the final disregard for Constantine's policies and for the peace accords between them, the two remaining emperors took to the battlefield. According to sources, Constantine by signs from heaven was assured of victory under the sign of the cross. This certainly added to Constantine's sense of call, and gave him confidence in every battle, which resulted in victory upon victory. Needless to say, as Gibbon writes, "every victory of Constantine was productive of some relief or benefit of the church."[9]

Constantine began with the Milan Policy in 312, then preceded to the Edict of 315, which exempted Christian clergy from all forms of public service. It also set up the bishopric as the magistrates to settle all civil suits, including those involving land disputes arising from the Milan policy, which had returned all confiscated Christian lands back to those families. Soon after the Milan policy had been initiated, Constantine sent a grant of money to the orthodox bishops of Africa in which he appointed Caecilian bishop of Carthage in a letter dated 313 to administer the fund

7. Gibbon, *Decline and Fall*, 2:68.

8. The Edict, in the form of a joint letter to be circulated among the governors of the East, declared that the empire would be neutral with regard to religious worship, officially removing all obstacles to the practice of Christianity and other religions. It "declared unequivocally that the co-authors of the regulations wanted no action taken against the non-Christian cults" (Gibbon, *Decline and Fall*, 2:69). This edict went beyond anything established in the past because it declared Christians as not just tolerable enemies of the state but neutrally accepted as subjects and citizens in good standing.

9. Gibbon, *Decline and Fall*, 2:69.

and to present the edict by letter to "Ursus, the most distinguished finance minister of Africa" to pay three thousand "folles."[10] After the grant was given, a group led by Marjorinus sent accusations to the high court of Constantine through Anulinus to accuse Caecilian of not being suited to the bishopric. This marked the first church schism by Donat and his followers, who included over five bishops.[11] It is more than likely that at this time Constantine started to develop his policy and understanding of the importance of church unity as security to both the church and to the Christian empire that he was sure to found.

At this point in time Constantine thought that the empire to be founded would emerge from the East and not the West. Theology and philosophy was the product of the old foundational Greek and Hebrew East and could not be a product of the pagan West. His hope that the church in Carthage would join the order of Eastern dialogue was founded on his support of the African Christian bishops with the grant given and also on the orthodoxy established by Tertullian and others who had so vividly and clearly defined the Rule of Faith established by the apostles. By the time he called the Nicaean Council, Constantine had marketed the theology that had emerged from Carthage through Tertullian as the Orthodox and Catholic position. It was his suggestion that the Creed employ the term *homoousios* to solidify a unity in the post-Nicene church. This connection to Carthage will be explored below when I endeavor to establish the necessity and the orthodoxy of the Nicene Council of 325 CE.

THE NECESSITY OF NICAEA AND THE CREED

The unity of the church, thought Constantine, was paramount in establishing Christianity as a major religion in the empire. By Scripture the Christians were bound together in love, but the fractured reality of it made for a tenuous peace. As emperor, he was obligated to the citizens to guard the Pax Romana and secure the citizens' rights and privileges in the entire realm. It was difficult to report success to those who supported his revealed call to be the emperor of a unified Christian nation if Egypt and specifically the Christian center of Alexandria was in turmoil. Rioting between the factions had broken what was once a testimony of peace.

10. Frend, *New Eusebius*, 287.
11. Ibid., 289–90.

The Council of Nicaea being one of the battlegrounds, Constantine chose to restore orthodoxy to the church. "My sole desire was to effect universal concord, and in particular to refute and depose of this question which began through the madness of Arius the Alexandrian, but swiftly gained strength through the wicked and destructive advocacy of Eusebius."[12]

Having been convinced by the report of Alexander that Arius had promoted a doctrine destructive to the faith of the apostles, Constantine convened the Council of Nicaea upon the realization that solution was no nearer after regional synods had failed. Unity in doctrine seemed to be the order that was needed to bring about a peace in the vital province of *Egyptos*. Some have suggested that Constantine cared little for accuracy in doctrine because he emphasized unity in doctrine to its exclusion. But I think differently. From the time he had received his "vision" for the empire, his focus was on the unifying agent of the truth. His obedience to the revelation of his conquering under the sign of the cross made it apparent that he would not take the traditional role of Augusta as being the "King of the gods." Dictating terms to the God of the universe was not in Constantine's role. He referred to himself as a co-apostle in his opening address to the bishops at Nicaea. This did not mean that he was elevating himself, which he could accomplish by right of Roman rule, but it meant that he was a "sent one" who was raised up to establish the rule of Christ. In Constantine's thoughts, he had been sent under the banner of Christ, who had clearly conquered the old pagan empire.

Constantine also surmised that his choice in sending Alexander to be bishop of Alexandria was a good one. He had obvious confidence in the school of Antioch over that of the school of Alexandria. This marked the first time that an exchange of teachers was made in order to intervene in an ecclesiastic setting and bring about an agreement of peaceful doctrine. Alexander was sent as the clear choice of Constantine, who weighed the evidence for him being the right bishop for the region. The several evidences show us that Constantine sought to know the truth of doctrine:

1. Constantine had put together a cadre of pastors to advise him and teach him, including Eusebius of Caesarea and Alexander, bishop of Constantinople.

12. Ibid., 352.

2. Constantine himself had been the one who suggested the Greek term *ousias* as the term to translate *substantia* from Tertullian's orthodox *Trinitas*.

3. He had concluded that *homoousios* best described the orthodoxy of the Apostle John's Logos chapter. The obvious conclusion is that Constantine had prepared himself by studying the church fathers.

Constantine had certainly seen the weakness of Origen's position of *tritoi theoi*, which represented the Arian position, and the truth of Tertullian's Logos theology as exegeted from the Johannine Gospel and Epistles. Gibbon writes of Constantine, "he prayed with the faithful, disputed with the bishops, preached on the most sublime and intricate subjects of theology, celebrated with the sacred rites the vigil of Easter, and publicly declared himself, not only a partaker, but, in some measure, a priest and hierophant of the Christian mysteries."[13]

As we explore Constantine's credentials and the ease in which he interjected the term *homoousios* into the council, we observe not only a military leader, but a highly educated emperor who with fervor explored the theological treatments of Tertullian and Origen and their contribution to the melee that was splitting the church. Both of the parties' originators could be seen and read in the Western church, but the evidence is that Constantine had considered their work and sided with the *Trinitas* of Tertullian. He then proposed the term *ousias* as the Greek equivalent of the Latin *substantia*, and proposed *homoousios* to sufficiently translate his "one *substantia*." It is clear that Tertullian set the stage for the Creed.

TERTULLIAN OF CARTHAGE: CONTRIBUTION TO NICAEA

The problem with Sabellianism is that it did not even regard the Trinitarian economy (house rule, that is, the workings of the Trinity in the world) as something to be attained or known. They argued that by recognizing the economic Trinity, the monarchy of God would be lost forever to the church. But Tertullian of Carthage (145–220) ascertained that the economy of God or his modes of working in history should be observed, but not to the detriment of the monarchy. The definitions of Latin terms that Tertullian employed are always to be seen through his ca-

13. Gibbon, *Decline and Fall*, 2:271.

reer as a jurist and a member of a noble family (Quintus) whose head was a Roman magistrate. Accordingly, Tertullian referred to the *persona* in the legal language of Rome as the mask in a drama, the role of an actor, the appearance, face, countenance. (This legal or jurist definition of the term does not mean "being" or "person" as we understand *person*.) Tertullian's jurisprudence background understands the *persona* of God as a division of the unity in the economy or by mode only, and as such the *Trinitas* is only to be viewed as part of the economy, and does not divide the reality of monarchy. As he writes,

> He must yet be believed in with His own οἰκονομία. The numerical order and distribution of the Trinity they assume to be a division of the Unity; whereas the Unity which derives the Trinity out of its own self is so far from being destroyed, that it is actually supported by it. They are constantly throwing out against us that we are preachers of two gods and three gods, while they take to themselves preeminently the credit of being worshippers of the One God.[14]

But he also stressed that the monarchy must not be dissolved: "I am sure that μοναρχία (or Monarchy) has no other meaning than single and individual rule; but for all that, this monarchy does not, because it is the government of one."[15] Tertullian elucidates the administration (economy) of the monarchy:

> Preclude him whose government it is, either from having a son, or from having made himself actually a son to himself, or from ministering his own monarchy by whatever agents he will. Nay more, I contend that no dominion so belongs to one only, as his own, or is in such a sense singular, or is in such a sense a monarchy, as not also to be administered through other *persona* most closely connected with it, and whom it has itself provided as officials to itself. If, moreover, there be a son belonging to him whose monarchy it is, it does not forthwith become divided and cease to be a monarchy, if the son also be taken as a sharer in it; but it is as to its origin equally his, by whom it is communicated to the son; and being his, it is quite as much a monarchy or sole empire, since it is held together by two who are so inseparable.[16]

14. Tertullian *Against Praxeas* 3 (Holmes trans., 599).
15. Ibid.
16. Ibid.

His impeccable reasoning starts with the solitariness of God as one of his many attributes as a monarch.

> There are some who allege that even Genesis opens thus in Hebrew: "In the beginning God made for Himself a Son." As there is no ground for this, I am led to other arguments derived from God's own dispensation, in which He existed before the creation of the world, up to the generation of the Son. For before all things God was alone—being in Himself and for Himself universe, and space, and all things.[17]

Tertullian then proceeds to incorporate John's Logos theology into the equation of the preexistent Son who was always. His exegesis of John's employment of *logos* is breathtaking and brilliant as he includes the Logos theology in the solitariness of God:

> Moreover, He was alone, because there was nothing external to Him but Himself. Yet even not then was He alone; for He had with Him that which He possessed in Himself, that is to say, His own Reason. For God is rational, and Reason was first in Him; and so all things were from Himself. This Reason is His own Thought (or Consciousness) which the Greeks call λόγος, by which term we also designate Word or Discourse and therefore it is now usual with our people, owing to the mere simple interpretation of the term, to say that the Word was in the beginning with God; although it would be more suitable to regard Reason as the more ancient; because God had not Word from the beginning, but He had Reason even before the beginning; because also Word itself consists of Reason, which it thus proves to have been the prior existence as being its own substance.[18]

Essentially, Tertullian understood the role or mode of the Son of God as a role of the thought and communication that God has with himself, as the Logos would dictate. Hence, he writes:

> Observe, then, that when you are silently conversing with yourself, this very process is carried on within you by your reason, which meets you with a word at every movement of your thought, at every impulse of your conception. Whatever you think, there is a word; whatever you conceive, there is reason. You must needs speak it in your mind; and while you are speaking, you admit

17. Ibid., 5 (Holmes trans., 600).
18. Ibid.

speech as an interlocutor with you, involved in which there is this very reason, whereby, while in thought you are holding converse with your word, you are (by reciprocal action) producing thought by means of that converse with your word. Thus, in a certain sense, the word is a second person within you, through which in thinking you utter speech, and through which also, (by reciprocity of process,) in uttering speech you generate thought. The word is itself a different thing from yourself. Now how much more fully is all this transacted in God, whose image and likeness even you are regarded as being,[19]

CONSTANTINOPLE: THE FORTRESS AGAINST PAGANISM AND THE BEAUTIFUL CITY OF A NEW EMPIRE

It was more than likely that during the council Constantine envisioned "Constantinople" as the capital of the Christian empire, the new Rome. He saw the emperor as a leading force to secure the safety and endurance of the faith. This could not be accomplished at pagan Rome; it could not be accomplished at any major metropolis in all the empire. It would take the building of a new capital, a city that did not have earlier traditions, a city that could be defended from within, and impregnable to the onslaught of the illiteracy of barbarianism. This would take a new city, one that was not, and now is. The village of Byzantium was the perfect site.

Before 327 CE, Constantine entered into a plan to dismantle pagan worship within the empire. His program included the removal of statues, other idolatrous images, and the wealth from the pagan temples. He ransacked the temples in Rome and sent the spoils to Constantinople. By establishing public art exhibitions in Constantinople he accomplished three crucial goals:

1. It provided Constantinople with the resources to build "New Rome."

2. The statues and other artwork removed from the temples made the new city a centerpiece of culture and inspired those who were colonizing the capital city to advance a civilized and aesthetic cultural setting.

3. Removal of the idolatrous works from the temples left them unattended, because there was nothing to worship.

19. Ibid. (Holmes trans., 601).

Norwich states, "Meanwhile all the cities of the Empire were ransacked for works of art with which the growing city was to be adorned." Norwich suggests, "since removing them [the statues of ancient gods in particular] from their traditional shrines and setting them up in public, unconsecrated places for aesthetic rather than sacred purposes, Constantine could strike a telling blow at the old pagan faith."[20]

During these years of construction, Constantine held grand triumphal ceremonies as the pieces of this city of cities were fit into place. The ceremonies marked an era of grandeur for the empire and for the church. The construction of several Byzantine churches (St. Eirene, St. Sophia, and Church of the Holy Apostles) provided jobs for skilled architects, artisans, and builders. Even the supporting economies involved brought wealth and prosperity to the city. Constantinople was becoming a world-class city. It is here that Constantine imagined a capital for Christianity, where all the learned Christian theologians from the world could come, dispute, and reach consensus and unity.

Large senatorial chambers were constructed with open courtyards full of the exquisite works of art and antiquity. Massive law courts were erected, and on the primary column entering those courts is inscribed "New Rome,"[21] marking the intention of Constantine in a reform, a reconstruction, a resurrection of a dead empire that was now new and pristine, no longer controlled by the petty and malevolent gods who had perverted and corrupted the old order. Soon, the senate class of Rome and other regional nobles flocked to the gates of the city to become a part of it.

VALENS AND THE PERSECUTIONS AGAINST THE HOMOOUSIANS (367–378)

Valens became the emperor of the East as Valentinian—the orthodox moderate—took the West. The bishop in Constantinople was elevated and declared coequal to the bishop of Rome. It was not a new declaration, but was an interpretation of several of the canons agreed at Nicaea that restricted and condemned the practice of one bishop usurping supremacy over another jurisdiction. The elevation of the bishop in Constantinople rightly balanced the power that Rome had so deviously usurped in the West with an equal power in the East.

20. Norwich, *Shorter History of the Byzantine Empire*, 14.
21. Ibid.

"Athanasius still reigned at Alexandria;" but the patriarchal offices of Constantinople and Antioch were occupied by Arian prelates appointed by Valens, "and every Episcopal vacancy was the occasion of a popular tumult."[22] Earlier, the Homoousians, having been fortified by Valens's declaration of stating that he would follow the moderate track of Valentinian, thought they had cause to rejoice. But having exposed himself in battle against the Goths in Gaul, Valentinian faced an untimely death,[23] and threw the East to the mercy of Valens. Gratian, the son of Valentinian, was only seventeen, and his-focus was elsewhere with the war in Gaul so that he was predisposed to ignore the condition of the East. Gibbon elucidates the attitude of the Eastern churches and the incapacity of both parties to live harmoniously with the other, however in separate communions, "whatever had been the determination of the emperor, he must have offended a numerous party of his Christian subjects; as the leaders both of the Homoousians and of the Arians believed, that, if they were not suffered to reign, they were most cruelly injured and oppressed."[24]

When the word of Valentinian's death hit the East, Valens was residing in his palace at Antioch, having left Constantinople to settle some scuffles between the two parties. Immediately, following the news of the death of the orthodox senior emperor Valentinian, Valens, his younger brother, took this opportunity to establish his authority by deposing the orthodox bishop of Antioch Meletius, whom he accused of Semi-Arian leanings, and taking a page from the plan book of Licinius, planted an Arian bishop by the name of Euzoius in his place. The act clearly put the emperor in a position to depose and appoint the patriarchs of the East. So, one might say that "as the emperor in the East went, so went the church of the East." Having taken this decisive step, "it was extremely difficult for him to preserve either the virtue, or the reputation of impartiality,"[25] and immediately deposed the orthodox bishop of Constantinople with a known Arian named Eudoxus who had been a long-time advisor to him. Unlike other emperors, Valens cared little for theology, and sought only to elevate his cronies and favorites. Having picked the group who wooed his

22. Gibbon, *Decline and Fall*, 2:544–45.

23. Valentinian died of apoplexy on 17 November 375, as he was in council with the Quadi who accused Rome of inciting them to war. However, he had previously persuaded his troops to recognize his son Gratian as coemperor of the West in 367 CE.

24. Gibbon, *Decline and Fall*, 2:544.

25. Ibid.

affection, he sought to make them happy, promoting them in every ecclesiastical favor and office. Gibbon describes the character of Valens: "he insensibly hated those sectaries to whom he was an object of hatred. The feeble mind of Valens was always swayed by the persons with whom he familiarly conversed; and the exile or imprisonments of a private citizen are the favors the most readily granted in a despotic court."[26]

THEODOSIUS THE GREAT

The demise of Valens came in war with the Ostrogoths in Thrace (378 CE). Gratian, still embroiled in war in the West, sent his finest general, Theodosius, to become co-Augusta in the East, and the Eastern church was able to breathe a sigh of relief. Theodosius assessed the damage when he arrived in Constantinople and concluded that he needed to deal with the Ostrogoths. Seeing that he did not have the ample military to defeat them, he called on them to parlay. He met with them in détente, conceding to them lands in Thrace as "citizens" of the empire. "By the summer of 380, thanks to his quiet diplomacy, the Goths were happily settled in their new homes and Thrace was once again at peace."[27] According to Ostrogorsky, the downfall of Valens brought about the downfall of Arianism.[28] That is certainly the case in the East where the bishops were convened at Constantinople (381 CE) to expand the doctrine of Nicaea and depose and exile all Valens's appointed Arian bishops. Gregory of Nazianzus, having been appointed earlier by Theodosius, played a major role in the Council of Constantinople and contributed greatly to the orthodox party in the fifth-century debates. The Arians were deported to Thrace, where they evangelized the new neighborhood of the Goths.[29] Theodosius heartily threw his lot in with the Homoousians and called on the council to uphold the Nicene Creed. Even as early as 380 CE, Theodosius deposed the Arian bishops that Valens had placed with orthodox ones. Eustathius was appointed to replace the Arian in Antioch while Gregory Nazianzen replaced the Arian in Constantinople.

---

26. Ibid. 2:544–45.

27. Norwich, *Shorter History of the Byzantine Empire*, 31.

28. Ostrogorsky, *History of the Byzantine State*, 53.

29. The Goths, Visigoths, and Ostrogoths were all persuaded by Arianism, and as they migrated and conquered toward the West, they took with them Arianism delivered by the sword.

The administration of Theodosius was particularly good for the empire. It is during his reign that the East can be distinguished as the Byzantine Empire by the codices of Theodosius, which brought a recodification of all of the empirical laws that had been so important to the empire. His administration was also particularly prosperous. Theodosius awarded the Goths of Thrace citizenship due to the service of military obligation, which entitled them to be land free-holders, which he called *foederati*. By granting them the land under obligation of military support, he bequeathed to the empire a full-time military power under his control of more than two hundred thousand strong. Subsequent generations in Constantinople developed an anti-Gothic political platform that legislated out the rights of the Gothic free-holders and turned them into mercenaries to send them away to far-off provinces. This greatly weakened the remaining families of Goths to defend their lands from marauding Slavs and Huns. Aleric the Visigoth was one of the leaders of the *foederati*, and after a rebellion of the hordes, he led an expedition of his people to the West and finally sacked Rome in 410 CE.

THE CONTRIBUTION OF GREGORY OF NAZIANZUS TO THE ORTHODOX CAUSE

Gregory the Theologian, as he was called, was a thorough proponent of the Nicene Creed. To preserve the Creed and the Homoousian theology, the dual nature of Christ was proposed and upheld in Constantinople and Antioch. Like Tertullian, Gregory was unwilling to sacrifice the monarchy of the Son of God to the economy, while still understanding the economy of the *Trinitas*. He reigned in Constantinople only a few years, from late 379 to 381 CE. His incredible rhetorical skills earned him a prominent place in the debates at Constantinople in which he declared the Nicene Creed. He was sent to intervene on behalf of orthodoxy by the Homoousian bishops of Asia Minor and Syria, and with skill of speech and clarity of thought he was able to declare with his orthodox party a decisive victory for the Nicene faith.

Gregory saw the debates in the church as going to new levels to preserve orthodoxy and defeat Arian incursions. He felt that the next position and debate must be focused around the Holy Spirit and his role within the *Trinitas*.

> Look at these facts: Christ is born, the Holy Spirit is His Forerunner.
> Christ is baptized, the Spirit bears witness to this.... Christ works
> miracles, the Spirit accompanies them. Christ ascends, the Spirit
> takes His place. What great things are there in the idea of God
> which are not in His power? What titles appertaining to God do not
> apply also to Him, except for Unbegotten and Begotten? I tremble
> when I think of such an abundance of titles, and how many Names
> they blaspheme, those who revolt against the Spirit![30]

However he emphasized the Spirit, his focus remained on *homoousios* as it applies to the Son and the Holy Spirit. He surmised that since Christ declared to the Pharisees that the blasphemy of the Holy Spirit was separate from blasphemy of the Son, the Spirit is indeed a third *persona* of the *Trinitas*. Yet he insisted that the Holy Spirit is *homoousia* with the Father and the Son, as he observed that the Scriptures plainly taught that the Father would send his Spirit (John 14:26) and the Son would send his Spirit (John 16:7). This he argued, "being two sides of the same coin." Certainly, because of the clarity of Scripture in the Gospel according to John, the Logos theology remained intact and became a template to understand the unity of the Trinity and the sameness of being that is the monarchy. "Gregory's middle course, then, is an attempt at one and the same time to assert the monarchia of the Godhead as well as to maintain the distinction between the persons of the Godhead, a balance that subsequent generations of Christians would identify with orthodoxy."[31] At times, however, Gregory's focus on the Spirit encouraged the followers of the heretic Origen to misconstrue his rhetoric as supporting *tritoi theoi*. Gregory used the word *theosis* to describe the incarnation, connection, and distinction between the Son of God and the Son of Man. But it has most assuredly been misunderstood. Gregory's use of the term was designed to explain how God could dwell in a human form without compromising his divinity or changing his holiness.

After the council and the apparent victory at Constantinople, he was able to return to his previous bishopric in Nazianzus. Having accomplished his purpose as patriarch of Constantinople, he could be the theologian and teacher that he was meant to be. One thing that can be said for Gregory is that the ambition of political power was not something to be

---

30. Gregory of Nazianzus *Oratio in laudem Basilii* 31.29 (Browne and Swallow trans., 321–22).

31. Winslow, *Dynamics of Salvation*, 76.

pursued. If power and authority was part of his lot as directed by God, then God would bring him to it in his season, but Gregory sought none of it and returned humbly and willingly to his office.

The victory won at Constantinople also put the churches of Antioch and Constantinople at odds with Alexandria and the surviving Homoiousian party there. In spite of all Athanasius's efforts to keep the Alexandrian churches in orthodoxy, the east African region still teemed with Arian assemblies. They bided their time and waited for opportunities to gain more power and control.

CONTRIBUTIONS OF JOHN CHRYSOSTOM

John Chrysostom, quoting from Philippians 2 says,

> This equality with God He had not by seizure, but as his own by nature. Wherefore "He emptied Himself" . . . "He humbled Himself, and became obedient unto death." "He took, He became." He took the latter, He became the latter; He was the former. Let us not then confound nor divide the natures. There is one God, there is one Christ, the Son of God; when I say "One," I mean a union, not a confusion; the one Nature did not degenerate into the other, but it was united with it. The union it is not spiritual . . . it is physical . . . because He took on the "form."[32]

Speaking of Philippians 2:5–8, Chrysostom says, "For by these words He has laid low the followers of Arius of Alexandria, of Paul of Samosata." He goes on to say, "Arius confesses indeed the Son, but only in word; he says that He is a creature, and much inferior to the Father. And others say that He has not soul."[33]

John Chrysostom also introduced into the orthodox churches the liturgical services that are in use even to this day. Another important contribution to the church at Constantinople and the orthodox churches of the East is John's pagan rhetorical education as co-student with Julian the apostate and disciple of the teacher Libanius. John used such knowledge and skills to debate and expose the polemic incited against the church by the rogue emperor. Even though the East had not taken Julian too seriously, the damage was done. John, therefore, becomes an important counselor and voice of comfort and reason to a church of faith that was

32. Chrysostom, Homily 6 (Broadus trans., 381).
33. Ibid.

taken by surprise at the intensity of Julian's persecution after expecting a continuity of support from the empirical state. John became a voice to sooth the harm done at the whims of a degenerate mind. He downplayed the rhetoric and exposed it as an illogical pursuit.

> John Chrysostom, a student of the pagan rhetorician Libanius, was similarly troubled by the rhetoricians' lack of moral commitment and by what he perceived to be the superficial nature of sophistic rhetoric. Chrysostom told his congregation that the pagan (*exothen*) philosophers, rhetors, and writers seek not what is beneficial in general, but have in view only that they might be admired; and even when they said something useful they also concealed that with their usual obscurity, as in a kind of darkness."[34]

John Chrysostom was deposed when a group of pro-Arian clerics gained control of the courts of Theodosius I and used John's preaching against him as a weapon against the peace of the city. The Alexandrian patriarch Theophilus and uncle of Cyril seized the moment to pressure the emperor because of the social upheaval that plagued the capital, and used it to indict John in the eyes of the emperor.

NESTORIUS

Nestorius was bishop of Constantinople in 428 CE and deposed in 431. Nestorius emerged from a monastery in Antioch having been thoroughly trained in the literal grammatical school there. Upon reaching Constantinople Nestorius observed the decline of the church in Constantinople after losing ground to Alexandrian theology. Nestorius saw the corruption of the monastic system in Constantinople and sought to eliminate traditions and vigils that were more akin to the pagan exercises of mystery religions and assigned a place with cult prostitution. The monastics that Nestorius countered in his new authority "would organize a service in church, and would sin during vigil meals by being promiscuous with women. It seemed prudent to Nestorius to forbid them their vigils . . . [consequently, his action] nearly exposed him to stoning by these women (and those who enjoyed their company)."[35] The disgruntled monastics of Constantinople later became a tool in the hands of the ambitious patriarch of Alexandria, who sent pro-Arian and pro-Monophysite

---

34. Wessel, *Cyril of Alexandria*, 184.

35. Mar Bawai Soro, *The Person and Teachings of Nestorius of Constantinople*, 514.

monks to Constantinople to disrupt the public order and peace that the city had seen.

"The Arians were not the only group that was targeted by the Nestorian Reforms. Sources indicate that Macedonians, Novatians and Quartodecimans were attacked on the charge of heresy and schism. Jews were also included, but the Pelagians, who were forced to leave the Latin West, were the only ones spared."[36] It might be mentioned that Nestorius had no reason to include the Pelagianists in his attacks because Pelagius's influence did not include the East. Keeping in mind his understanding of the canons of Nicaea, he did not interfere with the reign of other bishops, including Celestine of Rome, except where his emperor had directed.

His detractors, Cyril of Alexandria and Celestine of Rome, spread the propaganda that all sorts of disgusting heresies were hidden behind Nestorius's aversion to the title of *Theotokos*. Cyril and Celestine, by force,[37] convinced the council at Ephesus and issued accusations concerning doctrines attributed to Nestorius that were just not true and drew up the indictment against him. By wrestling the control of the council, Cyril was able to convene it early enough to obtain a judgment without John of Antioch and the other bishops supporting Nestorius. The council met without offering Nestorius the opportunity to defend his position, and in less than one day 139 bishops had deposed him, labeling him a heretic. The council itself did not condemn Nestorius, but Cyril added the anathemas later to the document.

The scene started when emperor Theodosius appointed the patriarch of Constantinople (Nestorius) to judge between Cyril of Alexandria and some bishops who brought a charge of corruption and heresy against him. Cyril answered in arrogant fashion, stating that it is a trivial thing that the Great Patriarch of Alexandria should be judged by a donkey. But in other issues Nestorius had complete right to question the doctrine of Cyril because it was known that the pro-Arian faction had several times sought to institutionalize the *Theotokos* as an object of reverence. Nestorius

---

36. Schaff, *History of the Christian Church*, 3:716.

37. Cyril blew into Ephesus with an army of over 500 and a supportive Egyptian bishopric of 50, and strong-armed the council into indorsing his write-up of its findings. It is stated that Cyril had even bribed his supporters to submission, and after, proceeded to Constantinople to bribe Pelchuria (Augusta) and Theodosius to support his anathema of Nestorius or else he would cause civil unrest if necessary (this is supported by Schaff, *Church History*; Kelly, *Early Christian Doctrines*; Loofs, *Nestorius*, 39–50; Gibbon, *Rise and Fall*, 5:23–25).

reasoned that if Christ is the *prototokos*, as Paul stated in his Colossian Epistle, then Mary could not be the *Theotokos* for it would make her out to be a goddess. "In the Syrian school, Nestorius had been taught to abhor the confusion of the two natures, and nicely to discriminate the human-ity of his *master* Christ from the divinity of the Lord Jesus. The Blessed Virgin he revered as the mother of Christ, but his ears were offended with the rash and recent title of mother of God, which had been insensibly adopted since the origin of the Arian controversy."[38]

Cyril remained neutral or leaned to Monophysitism,[39] along with Celestine of Rome, who saw the soul of the "Son of man" and the soul of the "Son of God" merging into a different single soul. Nestorius argued that the union between God and man would not bring any change to the divine will or the divine soul. Nestorius countered that to suggest such was heresy because God cannot be changed by new wisdom, knowledge, or experience. Nestorius surmised that the suggestion of the Logos being combined with a man, body and soul, producing a hybrid god was Arian and that it supported the Homoiousian doctrine of the Arians.

NESTORIUS AND THE LOGOS THEOLOGY OF TERTULLIAN

In the attempt to remove Arianism from the capital of the empire, Nestorius brought the Logos theology of John and Tertullian and the true meaning and understanding of the Homoousian Nicene theology. To illustrate the position and the concern of Nestorius for purity in the theology of the Byzantine State, Nestorius wrote,

> The union of divinity and of humanity in Christ is voluntary; how-ever, this union is neither moral nor spiritual, namely, the result of joining two separate persons together. The unity of Christ is not a natural composition in which two distinct elements are combined by will of an external creator. The carnation does not involve any change in the Godhead nor any suffering on part of God the Word, whose divine nature is impassable. The incarnation of the Son of God was not affected by a change of Godhead into manhood nor manhood into Godhead, nor by forming a third thing from these two *ousiai*; the divine and human *ousiai* are entirely and absolutely different from one another and they must remain so in the union

38. Gibbon, *Rise and Fall*, 5:21.

39. Cyril supported Eutyches, who was the Monophysite spokesman (Bruce, *Advance of Christianity*, 312–13).

if there is to remain perfect God and perfect man in the incarnate Christ; and so, if either *ousia* is mixed or mingled with the
other, Christ would neither be God nor man, but some new kind
of being.[40]

Arianism and all its future derivatives (Apollinarians, Monophysites,
Monothelites) were condemned by the anathemas of Nicaea but were restored after and gathered around a doctrine that Christ was not one in
substance and essence with the Father. We should look at Nestorius as an
apologist who distinguished and discerned the impact of compromise after compromise with the heresies given birth by Alexandria. Luther, having thoroughly reviewed the extant writings of Nestorius, validated his
orthodoxy by writing, "If Nestorius had lived in the time of the Council of
Chalcedon, he would possibly have become a pillar of orthodoxy."[41]

Nestorius forbade the title *Theotokos* in reference to Mary. He was
deeply engaged in opposition to Monophysitism and Appolinarianism
and fought distinctively against the Monophysite/Monothelite position of Leo the Great and Flavian of Constantinople. Being deposed by
the Council of Ephesus, all of his writings were presumably destroyed.
According to Ebed-Jesu in 1318, "Nestorius the patriarch wrote many
excellent books which the blasphemers have destroyed."[42] The remaining
works of Nestorius, according to Ebed-Jesu, are in the Syriac tongue: The
Tragedy, the Book of Heracleides, a Letter to Cosmos, a Liturgy, a book of
Letters, and a book of Homilies and Sermons.[43]

A wonderful account is recorded called the *History of the Bazaar*,
which details in brief the events of Ephesus as follows:

> The Council of Ephesus met in June, CE 431, and was dissolved
> in September by the Emperor Theodosius II without the two par-
> ties, the Orientals and the followers of Cyril of Alexandria, having
> come to an agreement. Nestorius was bidden to return to his mon-
> astery at Antioch, and Maximian was consecrated Archbishop of
> Constantinople in his place. In August 435 imperial edicts forbade
> the meetings of Nestorians and decreed heavy penalties against
> all who should copy, preserve, or read the writings of their master,
> which were ordered to be burned. By a rescript of the following

40. Mar Bawai Soro, *The Person and Teachings of Nestorius of Constantinople*.

41. Loofs, *Nestorius*, 21.

42. Ibid., 3.

43. Nestorius, *The Bazaar of Heracleides*.

year Nestorius himself was banished to Arabia, but he was actually sent to Egypt, where from a reference in Socrates he is known to have been in 439. But he was not left in peace in Egypt, for besides being on one occasion made prisoner by Lybian marauders, the ill will of his Egyptian opponents led to his being somewhat harshly treated by the imperial agents responsible for the supervision of his exile. In 1825 Augustus Neander, in referring to the citations made by Evagrius from a history of his misfortunes written by Nestorius during his exile, wrote 'That the work bore the title of "Tragedy" is reported by Ebedjesu, a Nestorian metropolitan of the fourteenth century, in his list of Syrian ecclesiastical writers in Assemani bibliotheca orientali.[44]

Having won the upper hand in the war between Nestorianism and Monophysitism, Antioch and Alexandria, Cyril then appointed the next patriarchs of Constantinople and Antioch. Through bribery and extortion he was able to bring the emperor to heel and win bishopric after bishopric until even John of Antioch was deposed and a Monophysite put in his office. But his victory was a shallow one, because all Cyril had accomplished was to split the church of Antioch three ways. No one really had the majority position because the church led by John supported Nestorian bishop after Nestorian bishop. The Monophysites took control of the church property, and the Nestorians and orthodox position moved to the suburbs of the city where they held to Nestorius's orthodoxy for hundreds of years. Even to this day the Nestorian Orthodox Church claims to be the true Antiochene church. It was not until the Council of Chalcedon of 451 that orthodoxy was restored to the East, but the anathemas heaped on Nestorius were not removed. In his apologetic work Nestorius defended his orthodoxy and his Nicene conviction: "Just as purple is clothing of royalty but not of soldierhood, and as the clothing of soldiers is the equipment which belongs to soldiers and not to kings, when therefore a king wishes to put on clothing, that is the equipment, of soldiers and to lay aside the purple of royalty, though [clothed] in the *schema* of a soldier of which he has made use without descending from his royal dignity, he then remains in majesty and authority over everything."[45] His illustration and use of the term *schema* parallels the apostle Paul in Philippians 2:8 and in no means can be misconstrued to mean "heretical." Yet none heard his

44. *History of the Bazaar* T. iii, p. i, f. 36.
45. Nestorius, *The Bazaar of Heracleides*, 21.

voice after his condemnation from the church. The council exonerated his theology but condemned his "Mariology" and left his anathema intact. As we ponder the real events of the Council of Chalcedon questions can be raised as to the authenticity of the written "Acts of Chalcedon." This will be taken up at a later time.

Below is a list of the patriarchs of Constantinople that includes the bishops at Byzantium before the construction of "New Rome" under the reign of Constantine.

Patriarchs of Byzantium[46]

St. Andrew the Apostle	
Stachys the Apostle	38–54
Onesimus	54–68
Polycarpus I	69–89
Plutarch	89–105
Sedecion	105–114
Diogenes	114–129
Eleutherius	129–136
Felix	136–141
Polycarpus II	141–144
Athendodorus	144–148
Euzois	148–154
Laurence	154–166
Alypius	166–169
Pertinax	169–187
Olympians	187–198
Mark I	198–211
Philadelphus	211–217

46. Square brackets in the table indicate schismatic bishops.

Ciriacus I	217–230
Castinus	230–237
Eugenius I	237–242
Titus	242–272
Dometius	272–284
Rufinus I	284–293
Probus	293–306
Metrophanes	306–314

Archbishops of Constantinople, 324

Alexander	314–337

325 Council I, Nicaea I, Arianism condemned; Nicene Creed

Paul I	337–339, 341–342
Eusebius of Nicomedia	339–341
Macedonius I	342–346, 351–360
Paul I	346–351
Eudoxius of Antioch reigned in Antioch also	360–370
Demophilus	370–379
[Evagrius]	379
[Maximus]	380
Gregory I of Nazianzus, the Theologian	379–381

Patriarchs of Constantinople

Nectarius	381–397

381 Council II, Constantinople I, Arianism condemned

St. John I Chrysostom	398–404, d.407
Arsacius of Tarsus	404–405
Atticus	406–425
Sisinius I	426–427
Nestorius	428–431

431 Council III, Ephesus, Nestorianism condemned

Maximianus	431–434
Proclus	434–446
Flavian, Phlabianus	446–449
Anatolius	449–458

449 "Robber" Council, Ephesus II, Monophysitism affirmed
451 Council IV, Chalcedon, Monophysitism condemned

Gennadius I	458–471
Acacius	471–488/9
Fravitas, Phrabitas	488/89–489/90
Euphemius	489/90–495/6
Macedonus II	495/6–511
Timothy, Timotheus I	511–518
John II of Cappadocia	518–520
Epiphanius	520–535
Anthimus I	535–536
Menas	536–552
Eutychius	552–565, 577–582

7

Conclusion

N O CITIES HAVE HAD as much influence on the church as these five
cities. From the beginning of Christianity these centers were the
driving influence on the historical, social, cultural, and political persua-
sions in church affairs until the demise of the Byzantine Empire in 1453
CE, and the beginning of the sixteenth-century Reformation. Each had its
own character and personality. Each had its own sphere of influence for
good and for bad. Each has also been judged for such.

We have observed the histories of each city into the sixth century. We
have observed the struggle for power and authority between Rome and
the conciliar churches of the East. We have observed the East's desire to
balance the power of the Roman West by elevating bishoprics in the East
to patriarchal status. We have also observed the affiliated doctrines that
corresponded to each city, which we will now sum up.

Toward the fifth century the imbalance of power led the emperor
to elevate some bishops to a new authority of metropolitan in order to
equalize the growing power of the Roman patriarchate. "Metropolitan"
was a title given to a bishop whose city had reached a population that demanded a greater say in ecclesiastical affairs. The title was directed toward
the eastern provinces of the empire: Syria, Asia Minor, Thrace, Armenia,
Achaia, Thessalonica, and the Peloponnesus. The Patriarch of Rome countered with the Archbishopric (*archiepiskopus*), and the Cardinal-bishops
(*incardinateus episkopus*), which corresponded to the ruling bishop of an
archdiocese of his own and a bishop elevated to a position on the council
to the pope in Rome, respectively.

JERUSALEM

The Jerusalem church extended over a span of three distinct and autonomous periods: The Jewish church survived from 30 CE to 115 CE. The Jerusalem Greek church flourished from 115 CE to 700 CE, when it was conquered by Muslims. Peter the Venerable referred to the Muslims as the "dregs of all heresies," and Islam became the most violent enemy to the church, executing more Christians than did pagan imperialistic Rome in the first three centuries. The third church period for Jerusalem was the Latin Outremer period of 1099 CE to 1187 CE, corresponding to the kingdom established in Jerusalem by the first two crusades of Frankish, German, and Norman militaries. The present work has concentrated on the first Jewish period, which had its distinct Jewish flavor and tied itself to the temple cult until the destruction of the temple in 70 CE. The contributions made to the church are hard to assess since the Jerusalem persecution of Saul (Paul) removed the Essene believers from the city and left the apostles to evangelize the Pharisees and Sadducees. However, Paul brought from Jerusalem the hermeneutics of the Pharisees, specifically that of Hillel. Such a hermeneutic was not to last in the church of Jerusalem, but took its roots through Paul in Antioch where it flourished and became a basis for an institutional school of hermeneutics, controlling the orthodoxy of the East.

Jerusalem's other impact was not on an orthodox footing. Ebionism and Jacobitism rivaled the orthodox Pauline authority held at Antioch and fought with orthodoxy on a christological ground. The Ebionites and Jacobites, claiming the apostleship of James the Just, reduced Christ to an adopted Son and a spokesman for the reformation of the Law. After the martyrdom of James and before the destruction of the temple, the Ebionite Jews fled to Pella and to Damascus, where they set up a network of antagonists to hamper the ministries of the Apostle John and Paul's disciples. Cerenthus was one of these who called themselves apostles to spread the word that Paul was an apostate from the Law and John had followed him. Cerenthus met up with John in Ephesus around 85–90 CE, where John responded from his 95 CE banishment to Patmos with his Gospel, his Epistles, and the Apocalypse. The Logos theology in his Gospel and his first Epistle is certainly John's polemic against the heresies of the Ebionites, of the Gnostics, and of Cerenthus.

After 115 CE Jews were expelled from their capital and the Greek church remained in Jerusalem. It lost an identity of its own as a Jewish Christian church. Being Greek, therefore, the patriarch of Jerusalem over the centuries was under the influence of the struggles between the patriarchs of Alexandria and Constantinople. This was certainly the case after the Council of Chalcedon in 451 where Monophysitism was declared a heresy. By the reign of Justinian, the patriarch of Jerusalem supported the findings at the Council of Chalcedon, and the Monophysitic Coptic Church had set itself deeply in the Alexandrian (Egyptian, Ethiopian) church authority.[1] This split from orthodoxy rivaled the orthodox party in Constantinople, fighting for control of Antioch and Jerusalem.

By the fifth and sixth centuries the Jerusalem patriarchate held authority over the metropolitans of Petra, Caesarea, Diocaesarea, Tyre, and the monastery of St. Catherine's in the Sinai.[2]

ANTIOCH

Paul brought the hermeneutics of Hillel to Antioch, which established the basis for orthodoxy. It appears that Peter opposed at first, having sided with James and the Jerusalem Jews. Soon Peter was convinced of the application of orthodox hermeneutics even to the Gentiles after a heated debate with Paul (Gal 2). By the time of the Jerusalem council in Acts 15, Peter had adopted views concerning Law and grace similar to Paul's. Early in apostolic times Paul and Peter faced opposition from the Jews, just as Jesus had, when they said, "How is it that you being a man make yourself to be God?" and from the Gentiles who said, "How is it that God would make himself to be man?" The orthodox church faced the dilemma in Antioch and won a great victory by the leadership of Paul, who trained the Christians to be not too Jewish, and not too Gentile. The battles in the near future were to be christological, and orthodoxy was required to answer the question, how is it that the Son of Man (humanity) and the Son of God (deity) could be joined together without losing the essence of either?

In regard to the Law, a rift formed over these issues between Antioch and Jerusalem. Peter no longer frequented Jerusalem, James tied the Jerusalem church to the temple, and Matthew as tradition has it, con-

---

1. Dowley, *Baker Atlas of Christian History*, 84.
2. Ibid., 84.

tributed his typological understanding of christological fulfillment as seen in the Law, Prophets and Writings to the church at Antioch which formed a uniquely orthodox school of hermeneutics influenced by Paul and Matthew.

The expertise in typology seen in Antioch derived from the Old Testament must be attributed to Matthew, and as tradition places Matthew in Antioch. The typology of Matthew must have been a welcome apologetic against the onslaught of malicious Ebionite and Jacobite doctrines that viewed the christological typology of Matthew and the Pauline doctrines of grace as a menace to their newly evolved Judaism.

The Pauline corpus of Epistles was added to the library of Antioch, which was Paul's home church. This enriched the city with a complete New Testament theology that was not influenced by the Judaism of the temple in Jerusalem nor by the extreme Hellenistic allegorism of the Alexandrian theologians. Hence Antioch was the stronghold for biblical orthodoxy for the first four centuries of the church. Antioch acted as the Center for Disease Control for all of the church. From the era of Nicaea on, the orthodox city battled as the war zone for the defense of the Homoousian (Nicene) party against the militant Homoiousian (Arian) party.

Compromise with the emperors after Constantine was the theme of the day in order to secure the peace within the church. However, those moments of peace were fragile and short-lived. The aggression of the Homoiousian party continued to be a nuisance in an arena where the true head of the church—Christ—had commanded love. By the fifth century and after the Alexandrian/Ephesian victory at the Council of Ephesus, Antioch was split three ways. The church of John of Antioch (Nestorian/Mopsuestian) and the orthodox position of the day were weakened as three opposing bishops emerged. The first was John and his orthodox church, the second was a Monophysite church established by the appointee of Cyril of Alexandria, and the third was the usurper of the bishopric who held an Arian position. The weakened Antioch church faced turmoil and discord, contention and even violence. By the sixth century Antioch was no longer the capital of Christian orthodoxy, but its emerging Monophysite church would not follow the lead of Alexandria by embracing the Islamic rulers. Antioch remained the front line in the war between the Byzantine Empire and its Islamic enemies throughout the seventh, eighth, and ninth to eleventh centuries.

The theologians of Antioch employed a logical thought process to test the Trinitarian arguments emerging from the school of Alexandria. By questioning the pattern of theological thought, the Homoousians were able to condemn christological error and expose compromises toward Arianism. John of Antioch, John Chrysostom, and Nestorius all sought to establish sound Christology that worked well within the Nicene Creed. An example of the logic went similar to this: If the Monophysite position is correct, in which the nature of the Son of Man and the nature of the Son of God are merged into one, then the Son of God has changed and his essence is no longer immutable. He then would not be God. If the nature of the Son of Man has changed then his essence is no longer that of a man. So the response of the Homoousians was that Monophysitism and all its derivatives had created a new being that was neither God nor man. During the christological debates of the fifth century the christological position of Antioch remained that the two natures are distinct and separate, and are in no way combined into one. The Council of Chalcedon affirmed their position as orthodox but did not lift the anathema directed toward Nestorius.

The downfall of Antiochene orthodoxy was as tragic as the life of Nestorius himself.[3] Whereas Nestorius was led into captivity by Cyril and died in the hands of Cyril's brother in Egypt under great duress and torture, the Nestorian Orthodox Church was persecuted and under duress from the Monophysitic Alexandrian usurpers, and they fled into exile to the eastern portion of Anatolia. But unlike Nestorius, the church of his namesake survives with a membership of almost a quarter million in the East.

The historical legacy remains intact: Antioch would always be the originator of the evangelical system of hermeneutics that was so much a part of the Protestant Reformation, and for the first four centuries of Christianity the city was the center for the apologetic to determine doctrinal truth from doctrinal error.

ALEXANDRIA

Initially, Alexandria's allegorical hermeneutic of the Old Testament was taken from Philo, and because he was a Jew, the Alexandrians who fol-

---

3. It must be said that the majority of patristic bishops appointed to the church at Constantinople were from Antioch and of the Antiochian school.

lowed him (Clement, Origen) sought to make the hermeneutic distinctly Hellenistic and separate from any Judaistic resemblance. In the pattern that emerged, the school attributed to Alexandria would compete with the Gnostics in its philosophic foundation but without the Gnostic tendencies that would remove them from the Rule of Faith. Clearly, the Alexandrian direction adopted sophistic dialect and rhetoric into orthodoxy. Such a move on the part of Origen clouded his heresy for centuries to come. Yet Origen provided churches with some of the best apologetics against Gnosticism and its derivations. The sophist philosopher and teacher of Julian the Apostate, Libanius, stated of Origen that he was the best mind of all Christians, but sold out to ignorance when he endorsed it.

Given the foundation of allegorical method, one might well say that nothing good for the church originated in Egypt. This truism can be seen simply by exploring those who were indigenous to Alexandria. With a plethora of heretics stemming from allegorical methodologies that left the church rudderless, the leadership of Egypt could only boast of Origen as a favorite son.

The theater of the Egyptian church was well known even to the enemy as Hadrian had stated in a letter to Phlegon his displeasure and awareness of the fickleness of even the bishops and elders.[4] It is not then surprising that Origen in his day was considered the pillar of Alexandrian orthodoxy in light of the crop of Gnostic teachers who dabbled in all machinations of sorcery and magic from pagan sources. The allegorical hermeneutic gave allowance to such teachers for "spiritual" purpose. This infusion of Gnosticism into the church, as Athanasius described, left the weak and uneducated without the truth. Even to the most discerning of Alexandrian theologian, the Rule of Faith was obscure, hidden, and could not be known (agnosis) except by special favor and mystical practice in asceticism.

Ultimately, Antioch was able to discover the errors of Origen's doctrines and declared him to be heretical. The key to uncovering Origen's christological lapse was in his treatment of angels. He stated that Christ was also angelic and therefore he had become the propitiation for even the fallen angels. Ultimately it was found that Origen understood the Son of God to be a created being and one of three in a unity of agreement rather than in substance with God and that his elevation to deity was by

4. Bauer, *Orthodoxy and Heresy*, 64.

an act of the Father which promoted the angel/man to an assistant god, not a supreme God. This set the stage for the theological wars between the two centers of Christian thought and brought to the Antiochene church much harm at the hands of a more aggressive Alexandrian leadership.

Origenism bred Arianism, and compromise with it on the part of sophistic Homoiousians bred Monophysitism. Arius, the presbyter of Alexandria, promoted and taught the doctrines of Origen by the numbers. Arianism or the Homoiousian party emerged, and its doctrines, which are described by the historians Socrates and Sozomen, were violently contagious. Having observed the violence of the regime of the emperor Licinius, Constantine sought to put an end to the persecution of the orthodox leadership at the hand of the Arians, and he appointed Alexander and Athanasius to lead the Alexandrian church. Ultimately, Constantine observed that there would be no peace in the church without the unity of the empire. The destruction of Licinius was necessary to enforce the Edict of Milan and the Edict of 315, which gave Christianity legal authority and preference in the realm.

Constantine's dream of church unity was never realized, and the bitter competition for power churned between Alexandria and Antioch. Through creating church political alliances, the leaders of the Alexandrian Homoiousian party were able to usurp the authority and wage war on the Eastern orthodox (Homoousian) bishops. By morphing their doctrines they were able to disguise the heresy contained in their teachings. Eventually the power of force came to play through the tyrant Cyril of Alexandria, and he almost destroyed the Homoousian orthodoxy by removing the two powerful patriarchs Nestorius and John of Antioch from power. Cyril was even able to badger and coerce the emperor Constantius into compliance with the two "Liar Councils," as they were known, which were held at Ephesus. Cyril's compromised position established the early stages of Monophysitic dominance in Alexandria, Jerusalem, and Antioch. Later this position of Christology viewed the Islamic conquerors as liberators from the tyranny of Constantinople and the Byzantine Nicene dominance. The Alexandrian hatred of the Nicene orthodoxy of the East left Christendom and Constantine's vision of a Christian empire in ruins. The dominant Monophysites created the milieu in the seventh century for the Muslim onslaught that destroyed true Christianity in Northern Africa, Palestine, and Syria.

ROME

The Roman church from its beginnings was wracked by pagan notions; this is surely why Paul and other church leaders were imported from other regions where the apostolic doctrines were prevalent. There were no native Italian bishops in Rome until after Constantine had envisioned a new start for the empire in Byzantium (Constantinople). After 362 and Julian's reign, the leadership of Rome had absorbed much of the machinations that the apostate emperor had in store for the church universal. It was Damasus of Rome who pushed the nascent Catholic Church and Orthodox Church to promote the veneration of Mary, to discard the use of the Greek New Testament and elevate the Latin text of Jerome as the "received text" in the West. The remaining churches countered the Roman church's unwarranted authority by balancing the patriarchal equation with the elevation of the bishop of Constantinople. Leo of Rome took the elevation poorly, and hurled edict after edict and anathema after anathema at the Constantinople see. Allying himself with Cyril of Alexandria, he approved the procedures taken in Ephesus. He confirmed the council's canons, which removed Nestorius from his patriarchal position and led to his death by mistreatment and torture at the hands of Cyril. He compromised the doctrines of Nicaea and the Creed itself with his *Tome*, which promoted a Monothelite Christology, which was nothing more than a reconstituted Monophysite position. He paid off the conqueror Attila the Hun with a large quantity of gold after Attila had destroyed the combined armies of the Western empire and Theodoric the Goth at Chillon.

The Roman Catholic allegorical method was taken from Origen when Jerome brought the hermeneutic to Rome having been firmly schooled in the Alexandrian method where he was raised. On several occasions Augustine sharply rebuked the leadership of Rome (the disciples of Damasus and Jerome) for resurrecting pantheism/polytheism after Rome was sacked by the force of Alaric. To disguise the Roman folly, the sophistic methodology was employed, the gods of old were renamed, and the responsibilities of the old Roman deities were ascribed to the saints in worship and prayer. Damasus elevated the veneration of Mary to new heights by demanding the doctrine of the "Mother of God," *Theotokos*. Sybil worship (the mother of the gods), which was the primary religion of Julian the Apostate, became a reality in the Church of Rome through the insistence of Damasus by replacing Sybil with the name Mary.

Conclusion

The ultimate goal of Rome was to recombine the secular and religious authority into one Augustus, or king of the gods, and pontifex maximus, high priest of high priests, so that all authority would rest on the bishop of Rome, thus restoring the empirical theology of the Julians, where caesar was god. Through the ages and by developed Roman doctrines, the bishops used sacramentalism and formed the pagan rites of old Rome and the ritual of the temple of Jerusalem into a ceremonial service that subjected by edict "all human creatures ... to the Pontiff in Rome."[5] The sacrifice of the Mass or "bloodless sacrifice" became the focal point of the sacrament of reconciliation (conversion, confession, penance). which provided an ongoing magical sacrificial system that Martin Luther called "priest-craft" that re-crucified Christ to atone for ongoing sins in the church and magically replaced the wine and bread of communion with the actual blood and body of the Lord. However, the Reformation of the sixteenth century seems to have been an awakening of the West to the systematic dumbing down of biblical theology as a method of control by the Latin popes. Where the Vatican controlled the debates in the West, the entire church of the East were theologians and debaters.

All regimes that have been totalitarian in essence have battled against their intelligent or tried to obtain the intelligent as a tool or weapon to forward their schemes. It was no different in Rome where the bishop sought preeminence and propagated a simpler theology that would subjugate the population to a doctrine that supported the bishop's claim to power. Allegorical interpretation allowed Rome to make the population dependent for salvation on the proclaimed "vicar of Christ" and "pontifex maximus" of the visible church. The sophistry of allegorical methods of biblical interpretation—confusing as they were—gave Rome at least the allegiance of the Latin West and allowed them to capture the Arian warlords of the Goths and use them as a standing army against all their foes.

Earlier theological debates, namely, the christological debates in the late fourth to mid-fifth century, played into the machinations of later popes of Rome who sought complete sovereignty over all secular authority. By manipulating documents of the councils and the Scriptures, the illiterate West bowed the knee in acquiesced surrender and turned the biblically mandated priesthood of believers to the formal rule in Rome. This soldier class of Gothic nobility came to be used by the popes in the eleventh

---

5. Boniface VIII, *Unam Sanctam*, 1302.

through fourteenth centuries to destroy the opposition in the Byzantine Empire. But it was the earlier Celestine endorsement of the crusade of Cyril against the patriarch of Constantinople (Nestorius) where Rome gained the most ground. The christological debate was suppressed, and Rome and Leo gained the much-sought supremacy in all issues of the church. Celestine bet on Cyril and stacked the deck against Nestorius by changing the field from a home field advantage of Nestorius to Ephesus—where Mary adoration was in a Diana/Artemis-of-the-Ephesians frenzy, and Memnon, the local bishop, was a known and established Monophysite. He demanded under punishment that the Western bishops not attend the council, and then appointed Cyril as the spokesman for the Western church and the champion of orthodoxy. The outcome of Ephesus silenced Constantinople and Antioch for over fifty years. Rome and Alexandria now controlled the universal church.

Did Celestine after the council dumb down the debate by throwing his support to Cyril? Was it the intention of Celestine to hold back the Western bishops in fear that they might support Nestorius and not his champion, Cyril? Fortunately or not, we can only conjecture here, but there is historical precedence to conclude that most totalitarian regimes seek supremacy by the suppression and destruction of dissenting opinions, and that the most dangerous opponent to a despot is the discipline of thought and academic freedom. There is no doubt about Nestorius's position on the gospel of Christ, nor is there doubt about his genuine desire to know his Savior and the Scriptures. However, was Cyril's assessment of Nestorius and his doctrine accurate? In a letter addressed to the Bishop of Rome (Leo), Cyril wrote, "I write of necessity to point out that even at this moment Satan is [through Nestorius] confounding all things, raging against the churches of God and trying to seduce people everywhere, who were once walking in the right path of faith."[6]

In the Latin West, however, over "the following centuries most users of the Bible made no distinction between apocryphal books and the others: all alike were handed down as part of the Vulgate."[7] Prior to Jerome's Latin Vulgate, which was not well received when first produced, Marcion's Latin translation of the ten Pauline Epistles that he canonized and the portions of Luke that he manipulated were used as priority texts. The

6. Quoted in Litfin, *Getting to Know the Church Fathers*, 247.

7. Bruce, *The Canon of Scripture*, 99.

only scrutiny that they faced was the introductions and commentaries that Marcion included with his text. In Rome, the anti-Marcion prologues replaced Marcion's contributive notes.[8] "But the vast majority of Western European Christians, clerical as well as lay, in those centuries could not be described as users of the Bible. They were familiar with certain parts of the Bible which were repeated in church services."[9]

By the time of the Reformation, Martin Luther was appalled at the condition of the church of Rome. He stated emphatically that no one in Rome reads Paul, or John; they read Plato and Aristotle as if it were holy writ. He proceeded to describe Rome and the profligacy of the Roman curia as no different from "dogs" that performed all their "natural," and biological "functions in the streets."[10] His amazement was inflated by what he saw in Rome, and he marveled that after 1,500 years of Christianity in Rome, the pope and his colleagues stood out no more than the pagans of pre-Christianity. The debauchery of the papal system and administration had made Rome into a cesspool, and the nunneries were nothing more than whore houses for the curia.

CONSTANTINOPLE

Constantine began building the capital of the Byzantine Empire in 324 CE when he defeated Licinius there. But the vision of building a Christian empire was foremost on Constantine's mind as early as 312 CE at the Mulvian Bridge, having received the vision some months before in Milan whole fulfillment was realized outside Rome. He proceeded toward what he perceived as a divine call. Immediately on the demise of Maximian, Constantine removed all the statues of the gods, shipped them to the East for demotion as strictly art, shut down the temples that honored the gods, built churches for restoring the security of the persecuted Christians, and returned all confiscated properties to the Christians. He also released all those Christians who were in prison and freed all Christian slaves.[11]

He knew that Rome was not suitable for the site of the stronghold of a new spiritual empire. Economically, it was unfit because all the wealth of the old empire was in the East. Militarily, Rome was unfit because it

8. Cross, *Studies in Theology*, 65.

9. Bruce, *The Canon of Scripture*, 99.

10. Atkinson, *The Great Light*, 16.

11. Socrates Scholasticus, *Church History*, 24.

was indefensible and had little or no natural geographical fortifications. Spiritually, it was unfit because every god of the old pagan realm had a following and a temple in the city. The social, behavioral, and theological baggage of the population was too entrenched to roust it out. In 326, during his last trip to Rome, Constantine closed down the capital, demoting it to just an important city in the West, moved the empirical palace of the West to the city where he received his vision (Milan), and returned to Byzantium to begin the construction of Constantinople that would not realize its potential for another three generations of emperors.

The village of Byzantium had all the economic and military resources required for the new regime. However enticing those might be, the village was not a regional center, and the city could be constructed from scratch, which made it the perfect site to incorporate the Christian infrastructure needed to facilitate the New Rome's being the center of a Christian kingdom. Constantine even had interpreted his calling from God as that of an apostle. He knew that his intentions were neither sordid nor self-aggrandizing, and therefore he had confidence that the plans would succeed. Succeed they did, because the Byzantine Empire never wavered from its divine place for a thousand years, and even though the church of Constantinople is in exile, it has remained stalwart to the Creed of Nicaea.

What was most significant for Constantinople was that it was new and uncluttered by the Roman pantheon. As a result of its freshness and newness, the city and its leaders established the Greek New Testament canon with divine authority. Constantine and his predecessors drew from the orthodox Antiochene school to supply many of the bishops who held leadership in the patriarchal seat of power. John Chrysostom and Nestorius were both bishops of renown who were brought out of Antioch to hold the bishopric of Constantinople. The authority of the Constantinople church rivaled that of Rome and kept it from the onslaught of Rome's struggle for supremacy. Where Rome endorsed the authority of the pontiff, Constantinople endorsed the authority of the Scriptures, and used the councils of the bishops to hold heresy at bay. The influences of the Roman West did not make headway in the Eastern Church (Constantinople) until the Byzantine Empire was in decline and sought military help from the West in order to abate the encroachment of Islam that had already taken the cities of Antioch, Jerusalem, and Alexandria.

Bibliography

Alexander. *Letter to the Bishop of Constantinople*. Translated by James B. H. Hawkins. In vol. 6 of *The Ante-Nicene Fathers*. Edited by Philip Schaff. Peabody: Hendrickson, 2004.

Ammianus. *Caesars, Julian*. Translated by R. C. Blockley. Online: www.luc.edu/faculty/jlong1/L388sch.htm. Print version in R. C. Blockley. "Constantius Gallus and Julian as Caesars of Constantius II." *Latomus* 31 (1972): 433–68.

Ammianus Marcellinus. *Res Geste*. Translated by J. C. Rolfe. Vol. 3. Cambridge: Harvard University Press, 1939.

Anastasius the Librarian. *The Genuine Acts of Peter, Bishop of Alexandria and Martyr*. Translated by James B. H. Hawkins. Online: http://www.fordham.edu/halsall/basis/peteralex.html.

Arendzen, J. P. "Messalians." Page 212 in vol. 10 of *The Catholic Encyclopedia*. New York: Robert Appleton, 1911.

Atkinson, James. *The Great Light*. Vol. 4 of *Advance of Christianity*. Edited by F. F. Bruce. Grand Rapids: Eerdmans, 1968.

Augustine. *City of God*. Translated by Marcus Dodds. In vol. 2 of *The Nicene and Post-Nicene Fathers*. Series 1. Buffalo: The Christian Literature Company, 1887.

———. *A Treatise on Faith and the Creed* (*De Fide Et Symbolo*). Translated by S. D. F. Salmond. In vol. 3 of *The Ante-Nicene Fathers*. Edited by Philip Schaff. Peabody: Hendrickson, 2004.

Aymeric, Patriarch of Antioch. *Letter to Louis VII of France* (1164). In vol. 1 of *Translations and Reprints from the Original Sources of European History*. Philadelphia: Department of History, University of Pennsylvania, 1894), no. 4, 14–17 Online: http://history.hanover.edu/texts/decline1.html (accessed Oct. 12, 2007).

Barhadbe-shabba, *History of the Fathers*. Online: www.cired.org/east/0303_nestorius_of_constantinople.pdf (accessed September 28, 2007).

Bauer, Walter. *Orthodoxy and Heresy in Earliest Christianity*. Translated and edited by R. Kraft and G. Kroedel. Mifflintown: Fortress, 1971.

Berman, Yehoshua. "Kamza and Bar-Kamza—Who Was at Fault?" Online: http://www.biu.ac.il/JH/Parasha/eng/devarim/ber.html (accessed November 10, 2007).

Boardman, John, Jasper Griffen, and Oswynn Murray, eds. *The Oxford History of the Classical World: Greece and the Hellenistic World*. Oxford: Oxford University Press, 1995.

Boniface VIII. *Unam Sanctam* 1302. Online: http://www.newadvent.org/docs/bo08us.htm. (accessed July 10, 2007).

Bowersock, G. W. *Julian the Apostate*. Cambridge: Harvard University Press, 1978.

Boyles, Deron R. *Sophistry, Dialectic, and Teacher Education: A Reinterpretation of Plato's Meno.* Online: http://www.ed.uiuc.edu/eps/pes-yearbook/96_docs/boyles.html (accessed January 27, 2007).

Brown, Raymond, and John Meier. *Antioch and Rome: New Testament Cradles of Catholic Christianity.* New York: Paulist Press, 1983.

Bruce, F. F. *Advance of Christianity.* Vol. 1 of *The Spreading Flame.* Grand Rapids: Eerdmans. 1973.

———. *The Canon of Scripture.* Downers Grove: InterVarsity Press, 1988.

———. *The New Testament Documents: Are They Reliable?* 6th rev. ed. Downers Grove, IL: InterVarsity Press, 1981.

———. *New Testament History.* New York: Doubleday, 1969.

Bucknell, Paul. "Origins of the Bible: Canonization of the Bible." Online: http://www.foundationsforfreedom.net/Topics/Bible/Bible_Canonization.html.

Chrysostom, John. Homily 6. Translated by John A. Broadus. In vol. 13 of *The Nicene and Post-Nicene Fathers.* Series 1. Edited by Philip Schaff. Peabody: Hendrickson, 2004.

Coogan, Robert. *Erasmus, Lee, and the Correction of the Vulgate: The Shaking of the Foundations.* Geneva: Librairie Droz SA, 1992.

Correspondence of Paul and Seneca from *The Apocryphal New Testament.* Translation and Notes by M. R. James. Oxford: Clarendon, 1924. Online: http://wesley.nnu.edu/biblical_studies/noncanon/writing/plnsenca.htm.

Cranfield, C. E. B. *Romans.* 2 vols. International Critical Commentaries: Edinburgh: T. & T. Clark, 1979.

Cross, F. L. *Studies in Theology: The Early Christian Fathers.* London: Duckworth, 1960.

Crouzel, Henri. *Origen.* Translated by A. S. Worall. New York: Harper & Row, 1989.

Davidson, Ivor J. *The Birth of the Church.* Vol. 1 of *The Baker History of the Church.* Grand Rapids: Baker, 2004.

———. *A Public Faith.* Vol. 2 of *The Baker History of the Church.* Grand Rapids: Baker, 2005.

Dowley, Tim. *Baker Atlas of Christian History.* Grand Rapids: Baker, 1997.

Downey, Glanville. *Ancient Antioch.* Princeton: Princeton University Press, 1963.

Drury, Keith. *The Wonder of Worship.* Indianapolis: Wesleyan Publishing, 2002.

Dunkle, Roger. "The Classical Origins of Western Culture," The Core Studies 1 Study Guide, Brooklyn College Core Curriculum Series Online: http://74.125.155.132/search?q=cache:http://depthome.brooklyn.cuny.edu/classics/dunkle/studyguide/sophists.htm (accessed 08/09/07).

Edersheim, Alfred. *Life and Times of Jesus the Messiah.* Grand Rapids: Eerdmans, 1976.

———. *Sketches of Jewish Social Life.* Peabody, MA: Hendrickson, 2003.

———. *The Temple: Its Ministry and Services.* Peabody, MA: Hendrickson, 2003.

Ferguson, Everett. *Backgrounds of Early Christianity.* 3d ed. Grand Rapids: Eerdmans, 2003.

Feyerabend, Karl. "ἔντευξις." *Langenscheidt: Dictionary of Classical Greek.* Berlin: Langenscheidt.

Frend, W. H. C. *A New Eusebius: Documents Illustrating the History of the Church to AD 337.* Edited by J. Stevenson and revised by W. H. C. Frend. London: SPCK, 1957.

Gibbon, Edward. *The Decline and Fall of the Roman Empire.* 6 vols. New York: Everyman's Library, 1973. Online: ccel.org/g/gibbon/decline.

González, Justo. *A History of Christian Thought.* Vol. 1. Nashville: Abingdon Press, 1970.

Bibliography

Goppelt, Leonhard. *Typos: The Typological Interpretation of the Old Testament in the New.* Grand Rapids: Eerdmans, 1982.

Greeven, Heinrich. "προσεύχομαι κτλ." Page 778 in vol. 2 of *Theological Dictionary of the New Testament.* Edited by Gerhard Kittel. Translated by Geoffrey W. Bromiley. Grand Rapids: Eerdmans, 1968.

———. "προσκύνεω κτλ." Pages 758–66 in vol. 6. of *Theological Dictionary of the New Testament.* Edited by Gerhard Kittel. Translated by Geoffrey W. Bromiley. Grand Rapids: Eerdmans, 1968.

Gregory of Nazianzus. *Oratio in laudem Basilii (On God and Christ).* Translated by C. G. Browne and J. E. Swallow. In vol. 7 of *The Nicene and Post-Nicene Fathers.* Series 2. Peabody: Hendrickson, 2004. Online at the Orthodox Church of America Web site: http://www.earlychurch.co.uk/pdfs/Nazianzus/The%20Deity%20of%20the%20 Holy%20Spirit.pdf.

Gregory of Nyssa. *On Why There Are Not Three Gods.* Translated by William Moore and H. A. Wilson. In vol. 5 of *The Nicene and Post-Nicene Fathers.* Series 2. Edited by Philip Schaff. Peabody: Hendrickson, 2004. Online: http://www.ccel.org/ccel/schaff/ npnf205.viii.v.html.

History of the Bazaar. Translated by G. R. Driver and Leonard Hodgson. In *Early Church Fathers: Additional Texts,* edited by Roger Pearse. Oxford: Oxford University Press: 1925. Reprinted online: http://www.tertullian.org/fathers/nestorius_bazaar_0_intro .htm.

Holmes, P. "Elucidation" 4 of Tertullian's *Against Praxeas* 5. *The Ante-Nicene Fathers.* Edited by Philip Schaff. Peabody: Hendrickson, 2004.

Ignatius, *To the Ephesians.* In *Apostolic Fathers: Greek Texts and English Translations.* Edited by Michael W. Holmes. Grand Rapids: Baker. 2007.

Jerome. *De viris illustribus.* Chapter 76. Translated by Ernest Cushing Richardson. In vol. 3 of *The Nicene and Post-Nicene Fathers.* Series 2. Edited by Philip Schaff and Henry Wace. Buffalo, NY: Christian Literature Publishing, 1892. Online: http://www .newadvent.org/fathers/2708.htm.

Jones, A. H. M., ed. *A History of Rome through the Fifth Century,* vol. 2: *The Empire.* New York: Harper & Row, 1970.

Josephus. *Against Apion.* In vol. 1 of *The Works of Flavius Josephus.* Loeb Classical Library. Cambridge: Harvard University Press, 1997.

———. *Antiquities.* Translated by William Whiston. Grand Rapids: Baker, 1974. Available on Word Search 7 CD-ROM.

———. *The Life.* Translated by H. St. J. Thakeray. In vol. 1 of *The Works of Flavius Josephus.* Loeb Classical Library. Cambridge: Harvard University Press, 1997

Kelly, J. N. D. *Early Christian Doctrines.* Peabody, MA: Prince Press, 2003.

———. *The Oxford Dictionary of the Popes (Linus, Anacletus, Clement, Eugarius).* Oxford: Oxford University Press, 1986.

Kittel, Gerhard, and Gerhard Friedrich. *Theological Dictionary of the New Testament.* Translated by Geoffrey W. Bromiley. 10 vols. Grand Rapids: Eerdmans, 1976.

Letter from Aymeric, patriarch of Antioch, to Louis VII of France, 1164. In "Letters of the Crusaders," *Translations and Reprints from the Original Sources of European History,* edited and translated by Dana C. Munro, vol. 1:4, pages 14–17. Philadelphia: University of Pennsylvania, 1896. Reprinted in *Readings in European History,* edited by Leon Bernard and Theodore B. Hodges, 105–7. New York: Macmillan, 1958.

Levick, Barbara. *Claudius.* New Haven: Yale University Press, 1990.

Lightfoot, J. B., and J. R. Harmer, eds. *The Apostolic Fathers*. Berkeley, CA: Apocryphile Press, 2004.

Litfin, Bryan. *Getting to Know the Church Fathers: An Evangelical Approach*. Grand Rapids: Brazos, 2007.

Leland, Charles. *Etruscan Magic and Occult Remedies*. New York: University Books, 1963.

Long, A. A. *Hellenistic Philosophy: Stoics, Epicureans, Sceptics*. Berkeley: University of California Press, 1974.

Loofs, Friedrich. *Nestorius and His Place in the History of Christian Doctrine*. Cambridge: Cambridge University Press, 1914.

Maier, Paul L., trans. *Eusebius—The Church History: A New Translation with Commentary*. Grand Rapids: Kregel Press, 1999.

Mar Bawai Soro. *The Person and Teachings of Nestorius of Constantinople*. Translated by Johannes Quasten. Online: http://www.cired.org/east/0303_nestorius_of_constantinople.pdf (accessed August 12, 2007).

McGuckin, J. A. *St Gregory of Nazianzus: An Intellectual Biography*. New York: St Vladimir's Seminary Press, 2001.

Midrash Tanchuma, Qedoshim. Online: http://www.faculty.cua.edu/cook/The_temple_mount.ppt (accessed March 9, 2006).

Mishna Aboth. Online: http://www.giveshare.org/library/sanhedrin/1.3.html (accessed Mar. 20, 2006).

Nestorius. *Bazaar of Heracleides*. Translated from the Syriac and edited with an Introduction, Notes & Appendices by G. R. Driver and Leonard Hodgson. Oxford: Oxford at the Clarendon Press, 1925. Reprinted Wipf and Stock, 2002. Online: http://www.tertullian.org/fathers/nestorius_bazaar_0_intro.htm (accessed September 6, 2007).

Norwich, John Julius. *A Shorter History of the Byzantine Empire*. London: Random House, 1997.

O'Collins, Gerald. *Catholicism: The Story of Catholic Christianity*. New York: Paulist Press, 1977.

Origen. *de Principiis*. Translated by F. Crombie. In vol. 4 of *The Ante-Nicene Fathers*. Edited by Philip Schaff. Peabody: Hendrickson, 2004.

"Origen of Alexandria." Online: http.religionfacts.com/christianity/people/origen.htm. Copyright 2004–2009.

Ostrogorsky, George. *History of the Byzantine State*. Edited by Peter Charanis. Translated by Joan Hussey. New Brunswick: Rutgers University Press, 1969.

Pelikan, Jaroslav. *The Christian Tradition: The Growth of Medieval Theology*. Vol. 3. Chicago: University of Chicago Press, 1984.

Pennington, Kenneth. "A Short History of Canon Law from Apostolic Times to 1917." Online readings for Canon Law 701, Catholic University of America, Fall 2007. Online: http://faculty.cua.edu/Pennington/Canon%20Law/Nicea/Nicea1-4.html (accessed September 2, 2007).

Philo. *The Contemplative Life*. Translated by F. H. Colson. Loeb Classical Library. Cambridge: Harvard University Press, 2001.

Ramm, Bernard. *Protestant Biblical Interpretation: A Textbook of Hermeneutics*. Grand Rapids: Baker, 1970.

Reike, B. "παριστήμι κτλ." Page 837 in vol. 5 of *Theological Dictionary of the New Testament*. Edited by Gerhard Kittel. Translated by Geoffrey W. Bromiley. Grand Rapids: Eerdmans, 1968.

Robertson, A. T. *Acts*. Vol. 3 of *Word Pictures in the New Testament*. Grand Rapids, Eerdmans, 1930.

———. *A Greek Grammar of the New Testament in the Light of Historical Research*. Nashville: Broadman Press, 1934.

Runciman, Steven. *History of the Crusades*, vol. 1: *The First Crusade and the Foundations of the Kingdom of Jerusalem*. Cambridge: Cambridge University Press, 1951.

Schaff, Philip, ed. *History of the Christian Church*. 8 vols. Peabody, MA: Hendrickson, 2006.

Schaff, Philip, trans and ed. *The Nicene and Post-Nicene Fathers*. Series 2. 14 vols. Grand Rapids: Eerdmans, 1996.

Schowalter, Daniel N., trans. *Panegyric of Pliny*. In *The Emperor and the Gods: Images from the Time of Trajan*. Harvard Dissertations in Religion 28. Minneapolis: Fortress, 1993.

Seneca. *De Ira*. Translated by Philip Schaff. In *History of the Christian Church*, vol. 2: *Ante-Nicene Christianity*. Peabody, MA: Hendrickson, 2006.

Seutonius. *The Twelve Caesars*. Translated by Robert Graves. Penguin Classics. London: Penguin Books, 1957.

Sherwin-White, A. N. *Roman Law and Roman Society in the New Testament*. Grand Rapids: Baker, 1992.

Socrates Scholasticus. *Church History from A.D. 305–43*. Translated by A. C. Zenos. In vol. 2 of *The Nicene and Post-Nicene Fathers*. Series 2. Edited by Philip Schaff. Grand Rapids: Eerdmans, 1996.

Sozomen. *Ecclesiasticus*. Translated by Chester D. Hartranft. In vol. 2 of *The Nicene and Post-Nicene Fathers*. Series 2. Edited by Philip Schaff. Grand Rapids: Eerdmans, 1997.

Tertullian. *Against Praxeas*. Translated by Peter Holmes. In vol. 3 of *The Ante-Nicene Fathers*. Edited by Philip Schaff. Edinburgh: Edinburgh: T. & T. Clark, 1892.

Thompson, Jay. "Limited Word Translation of the Greek New Testament: An Analysis." PhD diss., University of California Berkeley, 2001.

Unger, Merril F. *Unger's Bible Dictionary*. Chicago: Moody Press, 1974.

Von Balthasar, Hans Urs, ed. *Origen, Spirit and Fire: A Thematic Anthology of His Writings*. Translated by Robert J. Daly. Washington, DC: Catholic University Press, 1984.

Wallace-Hadrill, D. S. *Christian Antioch: A Study of Early Christian Thought in the East*. Cambridge: Cambridge University Press, 1982.

Webster, Leslie, and Brown, Michelle, eds. *The Transformation of the Roman World: AD 400–900*. London: British Museum Press, 1997.

Wessel, Susan. *Cyril of Alexandria and the Nestorian Controversy*. Oxford: Oxford University Press, 2004. Online: http://books.google.com/books (accessed Sept. 9, 2007).

Winslow, Donald. *The Dynamics of Salvation: A Study in Gregory of Nazianzus*. Cambridge, MA: Philadelphia Patristic Foundation, 1979.

Wise, Michael, Martin Abegg, and Edward Cook. *The Dead Sea Scrolls: A New Translation*. San Francisco: Harper, 1996.